MUSICAL INSTRUMENTS

PRANJAL BORKAR

Contents

music

Music does not always have one specific definition as this term can have many meanings according to who you ask. Music is many things depending on the musical style, culture, and the person being asked. Music is a language understood by many people all over the world.Music is the art of organizing sound to express emotion or put simply, music is an organized sound. Music refers to the combining of several elements such as rhythms, melodies, tonality, harmony, and scales in order to create a composition or song.Music can have many meanings for different people. Music can be healing, comforting, educational, and it can even inspire ideas (such as in the case of songwriters). Music is an integral part of most people's lives and it often provides an escape or a way to express feelings that otherwise might not find their way out.

Music takes on many forms and can be used to communicate different things; it can appear very positive and uplifting, or it can seem tragic and depressing. Music can make you feel happy, sad, or even inspire you to create something new. Music is very influential and it will continue to affect generations of people in positive ways.

Music is an art form that has been around for many years. Through music, one can express oneself and communicate with others. Music may have begun as a form of entertainment, but it can become therapeutic when people listen to it to help work through issues they are struggling with.This goes to show how powerful music is because it can affect different generations in positive ways depending on how it's defined and how it is expressed. There are many purposes and meanings to music; the definition of music can differ .Music has been around for thousands of years and it will continue to affect generations to come. Music played a significant role in the development of human history and was used by ancient cultures as a form of self-expression.It is a universal language that transcends boundaries such as time period, culture, age group, etc. Music is incredibly influential and people everywhere will continue to use it as a way of expressing themselves, communicating with each other, and enjoying their lives together.

Rhythm is the element of music that deals with time, specifically those elements known as meter and tempo. Rhythm has been found by scientists to be closely related to emotion and other psychological elements.Rhythm is the element of music that deals with time, specifically those elements known as meter and tempo. Rhythm has been found by scientists to be closely related to emotion and other psychological elements.What is music? Music is an art form that combines either vocal or instrumental sounds, sometimes both, using form, harmony, and expression of emotion to convey an idea. Music represents many different forms that play key factors in cultures around the world. A description of music, when asked by musicians, is quite challenging for them to put into a words. There is something unique, unto each artist, which music makes people feel a specific way in the world. John Coltrane described his music as, "My music is the spiritual expression of what I am my faith, my knowledge, my being. When you begin to see the possibilities of music, your desire to do something really good for people, to help humanity free itself from its hang ups. I want to speak to their souls."

Music is the art form that combines rhythm and sound to form a functional melodic line. Music itself transcends time, space, and cultures. Music can carry a mood without speaking any specific words. It can also be captured and recorded in a written universal language unique unto any other art form.

The history of music is a lengthy topic which requires much depth and time. Music is an ancient art form that began during prehistoric times. It carries with it a history for each human culture throughout time. Although there are many varied definitions of music, it is a cultural universal because every culture throughout time and history has made music a primary component of life. For ages, music was passed down through oral tradition on a fundamental level; but for formal purposes, recorded music began with the written tradition by medieval monks during 500 AD to 1400.

Monks used a written number system based on neumes which is a predecessor for modern musical notation today. This was also the time period when polyphony was developed, which means the usage of multiple sounds coming together to form a melody and harmony. The birth of music, as it is today, truly emerged out of the Renaissance time period. In the sixteenth century, a time period known as the golden age, began. The art of vocal polyphony in both sacred and secular music began to emerge and the theories on music were formulated. Gioseffo Zarlino was the Master of the Chapel at St. Marks in Venice, Italy. His work on proportion in voice and music formulated a harmony on the whole. The idea of balance in both the world and in music gave way to writing music with balance in mind. The word music is derived from a word in the Greek language, "mousike" which translates to, "art of the muses."

In traditional Asian culture, the instruments used were flutes and pipes, stringed instruments, and drums. The traditional approach towards music in Asia was through a methodological or mathematical terms of approach to writing and recording music. Throughout the passage of time, with the evolution of K-Pop music, this approach is still utilized in a more modern way. Some of the genres of Asian music include but are not limited to: Chinese traditional opera, C-Pop, Dangdut, Gagaku court music, Goa trance, Hindustani, Baila, Bollywood, Carnatic, Chinese folk, V-pop, Rafi, Raga rock, Punjabi, K-trot, J-pop, and Japanese folk music.

In regards to the music of the Caribbean, it is a mixture of African and European styles combined. The music of the Caribbean is a combination of music and dance because they work together simultaneously for this culture, which is why drums and percussion instruments are an essential part of the music. Some of the genres of the Caribbean music include: Calypso, Reggae, Merengue, Mento, Dancehall, and Mambo. Zouk, Soca, Ska, Salsa, Rocksteady, and Steel band music/Pan music.

Moving into European music, it is best demonstrated through classical music as a genre. Many notable classical musicians were from Europe and as such, the influences of their work penetrated into the culture. Music of Europe today is greatly influenced by it's peoples who have brought and appreciate music from around the world. Genres of European music include, but are not limited to: A capella, Celtic chant, Drum and Bass, Flamenco, Euro-disco, Trance, Polka, Grime, Opera, and Glitch pop.

Latin and South American music is often referred to as Latin music overall. However, there are many influences upon the music that influenced its melodies, rhythmic bass and rhythms. Some of the genres of Latin music include: Cumbia, Compas, Balada, Bachata, Bossa nova, Mariachi, Vallenatto, Samba, Tango, Reggaeton, Mesitzo, Mexian, and Ranchera.

Music of North American incorporates traditional American music and Canadian music. There are a wide variety of cultures that have influenced the music genres of this region. These genres include: Blues, Canadian folk, Gospel, Bluegrass, American folk, Industrial, Zydeco, Tejano, and Swing.

Music is made up of many components. These components could be classified as characteristics of the concept itself. The characteristics of music can be explained by organizing them into categories.

- Sound (timbre, pitch, duration, amplitude, overtone): Sound itself is defined as the ability to hear or feel a vibration of movement from a voice or instrument. The sounds heard can be articulated by high or low pitches; how long they are played for, meaning the duration; the volume at which they are played or amplitude; the way in which they are played and distinguished, meaning the timbre; and the layers of sound or overtones that can occur when multiple tones are played at once.

Melody: Melody is the line in which a musical piece is defined by. A melody is the central theme that is played in a piece of music and that is repeated throughout the song.

•

Harmony: Harmony provides music as a secondary line of music that compliments the melody. It is what provides the song with: color or enhancement.

•

Rhythm: Rhythm is the driving beat or pulse of a song that defines the movement of the piece of music.

•

Structure or Form: Structure or form in music means the order of each part or section within the piece of music itself. The structure of a piece of music communicates which section is played, how many times, and where music is repeated.

•

Texture: Texture in music refers to the melody, rhythm, and harmony that are combined in a piece which demonstrates the sound and quality of the individual work.

•

Expression (dynamics, tempo, articulation): Expression in music is the way that a piece is conveyed through playing it completely. It could be classically defined as the specific notes, the markings above each note or stanza of notes telling the singer or instrumentalist exactly how fast, slow, loud, soft, bright, or flat something should be played.

Music is also clearly defined by elements of the sound itself. Music can be demonstrated through speed or tempo, the volume at which it is played, tempo modifiers, and instrumentation instructions. The Italian language is the language of choice when reading written musical markings. A handful of of these markings are helpful to know when looking at a piece of music. Some of these markings include the following, but are not limited to this list below. All of the words listed are written in the Italian language and defined in terms of musical meaning.

CHAPTER TWO

Benefits of music

Music is a universal language that connects people all over the world. It has no borders or boundaries, so it's easy for us with our differences to find common ground.

This is because of its ability to transcend cultural barriers and connect people on an emotional level, which can be especially important when is trying to make new friends.

It also helps us understand different cultures better by exposing listeners who may not have been exposed before (or at least were less likely) to music from other countries. This creates empathy between groups through shared experiences like listening or dancing to music together.

Music brings diverse communities closer," says Dr. David Huron, adding, "music makes life more enjoyable." So whether your goal is making peace across nations using song lyrics written about love or uniting in a field at a music festival, music can be a powerful tool in bringing people together whilst helping to develop social skills.It's been proven scientifically, through the use of MRI scans and EEGs (brain monitors), that when we listen to or play an instrument, it releases dopamine in our brain. Dopamine is a neurotransmitter that helps control your mood, so this means you're actually making yourself feel better!

It turns out there are two types: "chill" hormones such as serotonin released during pleasurable activities like eating chocolate while others release adrenaline causing us to become more alert."

Music has both effects on listeners depending on what type their body needs at any given moment; hence it's great at helping you chill out when things are starting to get on top of you.

It has been proven that music plays a key role in brain development. This is because it helps with the nurturing of language, motor skills, and emotional intelligence.

It also has a positive effect on memory because it can help you remember things better by associating them with familiar or meaningful pieces of music.

Children listening to music from an early age can help with their language skills and improve their motor skill development.

The rhythm of the music also helps children develop coordination, timing and has been proven to help sensory integration, which is important for developing fine motor skills.

Music education at an early age will have long term benefits on cognitive abilities such as memory recall later into life when they become adults; this could be due partly to hearing new sounds but not being able to recognize what's happening visually, so are forced to use other senses more intensely than usual.

Music can also help children develop their language skills, as music and words are both made up of sounds combined differently.

Music helps with reading development, too, as it improves literacy by introducing a new vocabulary; when a child listens to or sings along to a nursery rhyme, they will see how certain letters make specific sound patterns that will aid reading development and phonics (the way we use our mouths).

You have probably heard the phrase how a child has a brain like a sponge that absorbs information. This is why it is a fantastic opportunity to give young children the opportunity to learn a musical instrument. They will pick up the skill much easier than adults undertaking musical training.

Music is such a big part of our lives. It is something that is universal and everyone enjoys from every culture. I don't think a day goes by where I don't hear some type of song playing. Music is a big thing that connects us all together. I love listening to music while running on the treadmill, walking to class, in the shower, and jamming out in the car. I've noticed that whenever I listen to music it suddenly brings me into a happier state of mind. My parents always joke around with question and me how I know all the lyrics of a rap song but can barely memorize things for a test. It made me wonder, what exactly does music do to us. It enters our ears but does something way bigger then just let us jam to it.

When we listen to music we are using our whole entire brain. Scientists are still trying to figure out how exactly music effects us as much as it does, but what they do know is that music has a very beneficial effect on the brain. One of the biggest effects music has on our brain is health benefit. Daniel Levitin, is a psychologist at McGill University in Montreal, who studies the neuroscience of music. Levinitin along with associates put together three experiments to help figure out what exactly is going on in our brain when we listen to our music. Levintin published a 400 study meta-analysis. One study was done with people that were about to have surgery done. As one would think, people are very anxious before getting surgery. One group listened to music before going in and the other was given drugs to help calm them. The studies showed that the people who listened to music were actually the group there were calmer before going into the room for surgery. This is great because music is much cheaper then drugs. Not only does music help with anxiety it also helps with pain. Studies show that since it helps relax people it is great for people who are giving birth or can even be given for anesthesia while in the room getting the surgery preformed. Another reason for this is became music releases endorphins, which makes people happy. These endorphins help counter act and distract people from the pain.

Music also can have a great effect on our immune system. This is because music makes us happier which causes our body to release immune-boosting hormones. This can also lead to have less seizures and fewer headaches or migraines because of the hormones and endorphins released by ones body.

The hippocampus is a part of the limbic system that controls emotion while the prefrontal cortex controls intense emotion. The parietal lobe is the area of the brain in charge of reasoning and administering information. Music has such an impact on our brain that it can even alter these different parts. Music is a great way for stroke victims to learn how to talk again.

Music also has a big influence on people's mood. Studies show that it significantly increased people's mood. When someone is upset, the best thing they can do is playing a cheerful song. This is caused by the body's release of serotonin. Serotonin is a hormone that makes people happy while also releasing the neurotransmitter, dopamine, which makes people happier. It is amazing how much music changes a person's contentment. Music can also make people more productive by putting them in a better mood. They feel more motivated and empowered.

With such a variety of music it's hard to tell which ones will change a persons mood. As discussed earlier, music changes people's brain waves and changes how they feel. Relaxing music helps people sleep. Many people who suffer from insomnia say that one of the best things they can do is listen to music. Scientists believe a person should listen to music 45 minutes before they try to go to sleep to help calm them. Pump up music like pop or electronic dance can even pump up people. Singing along to these songs also gives people more spirit. A study done at the Pennsylvania State University showed that listening to music really did change their mood by making them happier, more relaxed, or optimistic.

Although there is happy music there also is sad music. In one study preformed people were separated into two separate groups. One group listened to happy music while the other listened to sad. When they were done listening to the songs the groups were asked how the felt. The people who listened to the happy music were in a good mood while the people listening to the sad music were unhappy. The sad music also caused them to not have motivation to complete their tasks after.

Everyone is always hearing songs, and although we all hear the same song we all perceive it differently. This is because we all have different personalities and past experiences. In one study seventeen students listened to four different types of music. The students brain regions all acted the same but besides processing they all got different experiences. Sad music was sad for all of them but it brought up a different experience from their past, the same with happy music.

This also made me think, why do we remember songs from five years ago but we can barely memorize what we learned in class yesterday. This is because we have cement memory, which our neurons make networks with and makes us hard to forget them. This means a lot of our memory is filled with old music but since the brain consists of billions of neurons there is still room for new ones.According to Webster's New World dictionary, music is "the art of combining tones to form expressive composition; any rhythmic sequence of pleasing sounds." However, music is so much more than that definition; music is in everything around us. Music can be found everywhere in our world. It helps people find themselves, and helps them through hard times that we all face in our lives. Music gives us a way to express ourselves and show how we feel inside ourselves that we don't usually let people see. Music is important in our world, as well as in our lives, and here are some reasons why.

1. A Way of Expression

Music gives people a way to express who they are inside through many different forms. Whether it be being a musician (singer, rapper, instrumentalist), being in a band with other people, teaching music to other people, or anything that you can think of, you can be exactly who you are or who you want to be through music. Many people today hide who they are on the inside to try to fit in with everyone else because some people are afraid of being rejected by those around them. They hide in the crowd until they are alone and can be who they truly are without fear.

2. A Way of Communicating How We Feel

Music also helps people communicate how they feel inside when they just can't find the words to say it. Sometimes, in our lives, it is difficult to say how we feel to other people, but with music we find the words that are missing and the messages that we are trying to tell people. We all can find the words that we are looking for by either writing songs or just listening to different songs on the radio or anywhere we are. I know when I have trouble finding the words that I want to say to people, I write songs to express how I feel about them or different things in life. Music is important because music helps us find the words we can't say.

3. Music Brings People Together

Music can bring people in our world together in many ways. Whether it be through the same taste in music, or the willingness to try something new, or even performing music with others. Many people like the same genres or styles of music that are out in the world right now. Being a part of a choir, band, or any kind of group is another thing that uses music to bring people closer to one another as well. Music is important because it brings people together in the world.

4. Music is in Everything

Music is everywhere in our world and music relates to everything as well. Music is in all of our histories starting from the beginning. It is also in science and mathematics in many ways, as well as in everything else. Without music we would not have anything, life would be boring and dull. Music is important because it is everywhere around us in the world.

CHAPTER THREE

Tabla

The tabla is the most commonly played drum set in North Indian music. It is the instrument most frequently used to accompany vocal and instrumental music, and dance; whereas its primary function is to maintain the metric cycle in which the compositions are set. Though the tabla is essentially an accompanying instrument, the tabla players are also soloists in their own right, and many have vast repertoires of elaborate compositions handed down orally from generation to generation.

The tabla takes its name from the tabl of Arabic origin. The general meaning of the term tabl is an instrument facing upwards, with a flat surface. Scholars opine that the term table of the English language has been taken from the term tabll Some are also of the opinion that the term tabl is not an Arabic word in origin, but is borrowed from the Latin tabula.

In the beginning, the instruments which were egg-shaped or hemispherical, with skin stretched over the opening, which can also be called kettledrum, were called tabl. These were essentially martial drums, which accompanied the military expeditions of Muslims. Though made of metal, these kettledrums were originally derived from the pot drums of primitive men. Later they became rounded like the egg; this may have been an adaptation to facilitate carrying them on the back of a horse or a camel. Slowly it became a generic term used as a prefix for all types of percussion instruments, spread over in the Middle East, no matter what shape they are, i.e. the tabl-baladi, the tabl-turki, tabl-naqqara, tabl-migri, tabl-al-gawig, etc.

Tabla in our catalogue

As stated earlier, the tabla seems to have been in the beginning an instrument which suited the lighter variety of music and hence was very popular with the common people. It, however, remained confined to folk music and to the simple music of the lower castes, till the beginning of the eighteenth century. Around this time, with the downfall of dhrupad, a style of singing, and its allied instruments like been and rabab, pakhavaj also lost its popularity. A new style of singing, i.e. khayal, came up. For the accompaniment of khayal and its allied instruments like sitar and sarod, the need of a new percussion instrument was felt, which had the majesty of the pakhavaj yet could be played in a lighter manner as well. The tabla had the versatile tonality to serve both purposes.

The tabla might have made its presence felt in Hindustani classical music around the early eighteenth century during the reign of Mohammad Shah Rangeele. Sudhar Khan was basically stationed in Delhi, and therefore his school, or style of playing was called Dilli Baj or Dilli gharana. Later on his disciples scattered in various regions of northern India, and thus with the time span, several other tabla-playing styles came into being, but the source or the parent style of all these new schools remained the Delhi school. The principal tabla schools that emerged and flourished are: Dilli, Ajrada, Lucknow, Farrukhabad, Benaras and Punjab. Gradually, with the passage of time, the tabla acquired the rhythmic patterns and techniques of other percussion instruments such as pakhavaj, dholak, naqqara, etc., and shot to the peak of popularity in a very short span of time.

The tabla is an instrument of fingers, whereas pakhavaj is an instrument of an open hand (thapi). Therefore the rhythmic patterns which can be played on the tabla with unimaginable speed are impossible to produce in pakhavaj. Moreover the positioning of hands on the tabla is more natural than on the pakhavaj. A variety of tonal effects can be obtained by varying the manner of striking as well as by striking different parts of both the heads of the tabla.

The modern tabla has a highly developed technique of playing and in the hands of a master player it is capable of producing almost all the patterns of rhythms and cross-rhythms that a musician can conceive of. The well-established time cycles are rendered in terms of drumming phrases called thekha or measured beat.

The tabla consists of two drums, the bayan or the left drum and the dayan or the right drum, but the collective name for both the drums is tabla. The left is a small spherical drum, which resembles the shape of the kettle drum. It is made either of clay or metal such as copper, bronze or even a thin iron sheet. The right hand drum or dayan is made of seesam, khair, neem or mango wood, but preference is given to seesam wood. The standard size of the right drum is of ten-and-a-half inches height, the diameter at the bottom being about seven inches to eight-and-a-quarter inches and the upper playing surface varies between five to five-and-a-half inches. The left drum called bayan, is almost of the same height, around ten inches high, but the playing surface is about ten inches and the bottom is about two-and-a-half to three inches.

The goat skin stretched across both the drums is made of multiple membranes, one full and the other on the periphery of the full skin called kinara or chanti. This parchment, called pudi or chhavani, is tied to a plaited strip called gajra. Gajra is made by joining four or five leather braces made of goat or cow skin. Gajra is fixed to the mouth of the drum by means of leather braces called baddhi, made of buffalo skin. These braces are tied to another ring at the bottom of the instrument. There are sixteen holes or ghar to which the braces are tied at equal distance, giving the instrument an equal tension at all the points. Beneath each pair of leather bracing, a small tuning block of wood (gatta) is kept. In all, there are eight tuning blocks. By moving them up or down, the braces are tensed or loosened, thus varying the tension of the pudi, and the instrument can be tuned to the desired pitch. The most important and significant part of the parchment is the black paste called 'syahi', about seven centimetres in diameter; it is affixed centrally on dayan and eccentrically on bayan. The syahi is a finely ground mixture of iron powder, glue, paste of wheat flour and charcoal powder (some makers prefer rice powder instead of wheat flour). This paste is applied layer by layer on the surface of the parchment. After applying one layer the same is polished with a smooth stone, and before this layer dries out another layer is laid. This work is done by highly expert tabla makers and the total thickness is judged only by experience. Both the drums are placed upon rings made of cloth, which provide stabllity during playing.

The height and weight of tabla as well as the application of syahi, and making of pudi, all these procedures have modified and changed a lot during the past hundred years. Things have become more refined and the instruments are made with a more professional approach. The tabla is made all through the northern part of India but the ones made at Delhi, Mumbai, Benaras and Calcutta are of a superior quality. The parchment called pudi is prepared at many places. Each place has its own unique style of preparing it. Delhi, Mumbai, Pune and Calcutta are famous for their special technique. It is made in different sizes to match the different pitches of vocalists and instruments. While the tabla is placed in front of the player, the player sits cross-legged to play on it. The modern style of tabla-playing originated in Delhi, and subsequently it travelled to Lucknow, Farukhabad, Bareilley, Ajarada and finally to Benaras. However, some people are of the opinion that there is an independent style of tabla-playing prevalent in Punjab. Today, the tabla has become well-known and is extremely popular globally.

There are hundreds of artists who with their continuous sadhana and life long dedication enriched the instrument's technicalities and in its vast repertoire and popularity. Some unforgettable names are Ameer Husain Khan, Thirukva Khan, Habibuddin Khan, Ram Sahay, Abid Husain Khan, Anokhelal, Lateef Ahmed and Gudai Maharaj, along with the living legends like Alia Rakha Khan, Kishan Maharaj and Sharda Sahay. Among the younger generation Zakir Hussain, Sapan Chaudhari, Anindo Chatterjee, Kumar Bose, Shafaat Ahmed, Bikram Ghosh and several others are the prominent tabla players that India has produced.

tabla, pair of small drums fundamental (since the 18th century) to Hindustani music of northern India, Pakistan, and Bangladesh. The higher-pitched of the two drums, which is played with the right hand, is also referred to individually as the tabla or as the daya (dahina or dayan, meaning "right"). It is a single-headed drum usually of wood and having the profile of two truncated cones bulging at the centre, the lower portion shorter. It is about 25 cm (10 inches) in height and 15 cm (6 inches) across. Skin tension is maintained by thong lacings and wooden dowels that are tapped with a hammer in retuning. It is usually tuned to the tonic, or ground note, of the raga (melodic framework).

The baya (bahina or bayan, meaning "left"), played with the left hand, is a deep kettledrum measuring about 25 cm (10 inches) in height, and the drum face is about 20 cm (8 inches) in diameter. It is usually made of copper but may also be made of clay or wood, with a hoop and thong lacings to maintain skin tension. Pressure from the heel of the player's hand changes the tone colour and pitch. The tuning of the baya varies, but it may be a fifth or an octave below the daya. A disk of black tuning paste placed on the skin of each drum affects pitch and also generates overtones characteristic of the drums' sound. The musician plays the tabla while seated, with the baya to the left of the daya. Sound is produced on the drums through a variety of different finger and hand strokes. Each drum stroke can be expressed by a corresponding syllable, used for both teaching and performance purposes. The intricate music of the drums reflects the rhythmic framework (tala) of the piece.

This theory is based on the etymological links of the word tabla to Arabic word tabl which means "drum". Beyond the root of the word, this proposal points to the documentary evidence that the Muslim armies had hundreds of soldiers on camels and horses carrying paired drums as they invaded the Indian subcontinent. They would beat these drums to scare the residents, the non-Muslim armies, their elephants and chariots, that they intended to attack. However, the war drums did not look or sound anything like tabla, they were large paired drums and were called naqqara (noise, chaos makers).

Another version states that Amir Khusraw, a musician patronized by Sultan Alauddin Khalji invented the tabla when he cut an Awaj drum, which used to be hourglass shaped, into two parts. However, no painting or sculpture or document dated to his period supports it with this evidence nor it was found in the list of musical instruments that were written down by Muslim historians. For example, Abul Fazi included a long list of musical instruments in his Ain-i-akbari written in the time of the 16th century Mughal Emperor Akbar, the generous patron of music. Abul Fazi's list makes no mention of tabla.

The third version credits the invention of tabla to the 18th century musician, with a similar sounding name Amir Khusru, where he is suggested to have cut a Pakhawaj into two to create tabla. Miniature paintings of this era show instruments that sort of look like tabla. This theory implies that tabla emerged from within the Muslim community of Indian subcontinent and were not an Arabian import. However, scholars such as Neil Sorrell and Ram Narayan state that this legend of cutting a pakhawaj drum into two to make tabla drums "cannot be given any credence".

Indian music is traditionally practice-oriented and until the 20th century did not employ written notations as the primary media of instruction, understanding, or transmission. The rules of Indian music and compositions themselves are taught from a guru to a shishya, in person. Thus oral notation for playing tabla strokes and compositions is very developed and exact. These are made up of onomatopoetic syllables and are known as bols.

Written notation is regarded as a matter of taste and is not standardized. Thus there is no universal system of written notation for the rest of the world to study Indian music. The two popular systems for writing notations were created by Vishnu Digambar Paluskar and Vishnu Narayan Bhatkhande. These notations are named after their respective creators. Both these systems have bols written down in a script such as Latin or Devanagari. The differences arise in representation of various concepts of a compositions, such as Taali, Khaali, Sum (the first beat in a rhythmic cycle), and Khand (divisions). Another difference is the use of numerals in the Vishnu Narayan Bhatkande system to represent matras and beat measures, whereas more sophisticated symbols are used in the Vishnu Digambar Paluskar system to denote one matra, its fractions and combinations.

Tabla's repertoire and techniques borrow many elements from Pakhavaj and Mridangam, which are played sideways using one's palms. The physical structure of these drums also share similar components: the smaller pakhavaj head for the dayan, the naqqara kettledrum for the bayan, and the flexible use of the bass of the dholak. Tabla is played from the top and uses "finger tip and hand percussive" techniques allowing more complex movements.The rich language of tabla is made up of permutations of some basic strokes. These basic strokes are divided into 5 major categories along with a few examples:

Bols played on the dayan (right / treble drum)

Na: striking the edge of the syahi with the last two fingers of the right hand

Ta or Ra: striking sharply with the index finger against the rim while simultaneously applying gentle pressure to the edge of the syahi with the ring finger to suppress the fundamental vibration mode

Tin: placing the last two fingers of the right hand lightly against the syahi and striking on the border between the syahi and the maidan (resonant)

Te: striking the center of the syahi with the middle finger in Delhi gharana, or using middle, ring, and little fingers together in Varanasi style (non resonant)

Ti: striking the center of the syahi with the index finger (non resonant)

Tun: striking the center of the syahi with the index finger to excite the fundamental vibration mode (resonant)

TheRe: striking of syahi with palm

Bols played on bayan (left / bass drum)

Ghe: holding wrist down and arching the fingers over the syahi; the middle and ring-fingers then strike the maidan (resonant)

Ga: striking the index finger

Ka, Ke, or Kat: (on bayan) striking with the flat palm and fingers (non resonant)

Bols played on both the drums on unison

Dha: combination of Na and (Ga or Ghe)

Dhin: combination of Tin and (Ga or Ghe)

Bols played one after another in a successive manner

Ti Re Ki Ta

TaK = Ta + Ke

Bols played as flam

Ghran: Ge immediately followed by Na

TriKe: Ti immediately followed by Ke and Te

Tabla Talas

Tala defines the musical meter of a composition. It is characterized by groups of matras in a defined time cycle.Talas are composed of basic elements, bols. Matra defines the number of beats within a rhythm. Talas can be of 3 to 108 matras. They are played in repeated cycles. The starting beat of each cycle is known as Sum. This beat is often represented by a special symbol such as 'X'. This is the most emphasized beat of the cycle. Other emphasized parts of the tala which are represented by Taali (clap), while Khali (empty) portions are played in a relaxed manner. They are represented by a 'O' in Vishnu Narayanan Bhatkhande notation. Tali is often marked by a numeral representing its beat measure. Separate sections or stanzas of a tala are called Vibhagas.

Three main types of tempos or layas are used in playing Tabla talas: 1) Slow (vilambit) or half speed, 2) Medium (madhya) or reference speed, and 3) Fast (drut) or double speed. Keeping these three tempos as reference other variations of these tempos are also defined such as Aadi laya where bols are played at one and a half speed of medium tempo. Others such as Ati Ati drut laya stands for very very fast tempo. Modern tabla players often use beats per minute measures as well.

CHAPTER FOUR

Sitar

Sitar, stringed instrument of the lute family that is popular in northern India, Pakistan, and Bangladesh. Typically measuring about 1.2 metres (4 feet) in length, the sitar has a deep pear-shaped gourd body; a long, wide, hollow wooden neck; both front and side tuning pegs; and 20 arched movable frets. Its strings are metal; there are usually five melody strings, one or two drone strings used to accentuate the rhythm or pulse, and as many as 13 sympathetic strings beneath the frets in the neck that are tuned to the notes of the raga (melodic framework of the performance). The convex metal frets are tied along the neck, which enables them to be moved as needed. The sitar often has a resonating gourd under the pegbox end of the neck; this balances the weight of the instrument and helps support it when it is not being played. Musicians hold the sitar at a 45° angle on their laps while seated. They pluck the strings with a wire plectrum worn on the right forefinger while the left hand manipulates the strings with subtle pressure on or between the frets and with sideways pulls of the strings.

The word sitar is derived from the Persian word sehtar, meaning "three-stringed." The instrument appears to have descended from long-necked lutes taken to India from Central Asia. The sitar flourished in the 16th and 17th centuries and arrived at its present form in the 18th century. Today it is the dominant instrument in Hindustani music;

it is used as a solo instrument with tambura (drone-lute) and tabla (drums) and in ensembles, as well as for northern Indian kathak (dance-dramas). Two modern schools of sitar playing in India are the Ravi Shankar and Vilayat Khan schools, each with its own playing style, type of sitar (varying in size, shape, number of strings, etc.), and tuning system.

The sitar (English: /'s I t ɑ ː r/ or /s I 't ɑ ː r/; IAST: sitāra) is a plucked stringed instrument, originating from the Indian subcontinent, used in Hindustani classical music. The instrument was invented in medieval India, flourished in the 18th century, and arrived at its present form in 19th-century India. Khusrau Khan, an 18th century figure of Mughal India has been identified by modern scholarship as the originator of Sitar. According to most historians he developed sitar from setar, an Iranian instrument of Abbasid or Safavid origin. Another view supported by a minority of scholars is that Khsrau Khan developed it from Veena.

Used widely throughout the Indian subcontinent, the sitar became popularly known in the wider world through the works of Ravi Shankar, beginning in the late 1950s and early 1960s.In the 1960s, a short-lived trend arose for the use of the sitar in Western popular music, with the instrument appearing on tracks by bands such as the Beatles, the Doors, the Rolling Stones and others.

The book "The New Grove Dictionary of Music and Musicians" suggests possibility of the sitar's origin as that evolved from one or more instruments of the tanbūr family, long necked lutes which it argues were introduced and popularised during the period of Mughal rule. Allyn

Miner, a concert performer and a Senior Lecturer in the Department of South Asia Studies at the University of Pennsylvania suggests that the evidence of indigenous long-necked lutes in India is particularly lacking.According to this view, when Muslim rule began in Northern India in 1192, the conquerors brought with them tanbur-family instruments, and other instruments in their "multi-national" army. In this early period, the Muslim instrument was linked to the tradition of Sufi ecstatic dance, "sufiānā rang".

It was also theorized in Muslim tradition, that the sitar was invented, or rather developed by Amir Khusrow (c. 1253–1325), a famous Sufi inventor, poet and pioneer of Khyal, Tarana and Qawwali, during the 13th century. However, the tradition of Amir Khusrow is considered discredited by some scholars. Whatever instruments he might have played, no record exists from this period using the name "sitar".

Another, more minor hypothesis is that the sitar is derived from locally developed Indian instruments, such as the veena, prior to the arrival of Islam. Indian temple sculptures from the 9th and 10th centuries are known to feature sitar-like instruments. However, according to Allyn Miner, the evidence for this theory is too weak for any conclusion.

In the early Mughal Empire (1526–1707), tanbur-style instruments continued to be used in court[citation needed]. They were beginning to change; in images from the period, an instrument resembling an Uzbek dutar or a tambūrā is being played on the shoulder, with the "deep bridge of the modern sitar and the tambūrā". Looking at the musicians (the way they played their instruments in surviving images, their identities that were recorded) led historian Alastair Dick to conclude that the instrument was being adopted for Hindu music by Hindu musicians. The instrument was used for "Persian and Hindu melodies". According to Dick, the "modern view that ... invading Muslims simply changed into Persian the name of an existing Hindu instrument ... has no historical or musical foundation".

In the late Mughal Empire (1707–1858), the instrument began to take on its modern shape. The neck got wider. The bowl, which had been made of glued lathes of wood was now made of gourd, with metal frets and a bone nut on the neck.

By about 1725, the name sitar was used in the Hammir-raso by Jodhraj, a Rajasthan author. The instrument had 5 strings by this time. The beginnings of the modern 7-string tuning were present too.

A sitar can have 18, 19, 20, or 21 strings; 6 or 7 of these run over curved, raised frets and are played strings; the remainder are sympathetic strings (tarb, also known as taarif or tarafdaar), running underneath the frets and resonating in sympathy with the played strings. These strings are generally used to set the mood of a raga at the very beginning of a presentation. The frets, which are known as pardā or that, are movable, allowing fine tuning. The played strings run to tuning pegs on or near the head of the instrument, while the sympathetic strings, which have a variety of different lengths, pass through small holes in the fretboard to engage with the smaller tuning pegs that run down the instrument's neck.

The instrument has two bridges: the large bridge (badaa goraa) for the playing and drone strings and the small bridge (chota goraa) for the sympathetic strings. Its timbre results from the way the strings interact with the wide, rounded bridge. As a string vibrates, its length changes slightly as one edge moves along the rounded bridge, promoting the creation of overtones and giving the sound its distinctive tone.The maintenance of this specific tone by shaping the bridge is called jawari. Many musicians rely on instrument makers to adjust this.

Materials used in construction include teak wood or tun wood (Cedrela toona), which is a variation of mahogany, for the neck and faceplate (tabli), and calabash gourds for the resonating chambers. The instrument's bridges are made of deer horn, ebony, or very occasionally from camel bone. Synthetic material is now common as well.

There are two popular modern styles of sitar: the fully decorated "instrumental style" (sometimes called the "Ravi Shankar style") and the "gayaki" style (sometimes called the "Vilayat Khan" style).

Close-up of the pen work on a "Ravi Shankar style" sitar

The instrumental style sitar is most often made of seasoned toon wood, but sometimes made of Burma teak. It is often fitted with a second resonator, a small tumba (pumpkin or pumpkin-like wood replica) on the neck. This style is usually fully decorated, with floral or grape carvings and celluloid inlays with colored (often brown or red) and black floral or arabesque patterns. It typically has 13 sympathetic strings. It is said that the best Burma teak sitars are made from teak that has been seasoned for generations. Therefore, instrument builders look for old Burma teak that was used in old colonial-style villas as whole trunk columns for their special sitar constructions. The sources of very old seasoned wood are a highly guarded trade secret and sometimes a mystery.

Preferences of taraf string and peg positioning and their total number

There are various additional sub-styles and cross mixes of styles in sitars, according to customer preferences. Most importantly, there are some differences in preferences for the positioning of sympathetic (taraf) string pegs (see photo).

Amongst all sitar styles, there are student styles, beginner models, semi-pro styles, pro-models, master models, and so on. Prices are often determined by the manufacturer's name and not by looks alone or materials used. Some sitars by certain manufacturers fetch very high collectible prices. Most notable are older Rikhi Ram (Delhi) and older Hiren Roy (Kolkata) sitars, depending upon which master built the instrument. Nikhil Banerjee had a small extra bridge fixed at the top of the Sitar fingerboard for sustenance of sound.

Tuning depends on the sitarist's school or style, tradition and each artist's personal preference. The main playing string is almost invariably tuned a perfect fourth above the tonic, the second string being tuned to the tonic. The tonic in the Indian solfège system is referred to as ṣaḍja, ṣaḍaj, or the shortened form sa, or khaṛaj, a dialectal variant of ṣaḍaj, not as vād, and the perfect fifth to which one or more of the drones strings are tuned is referred to as pañcam, not samvād.

(The last three in the upper octave).[clarify] The player should re-tune for each raga. Strings are tuned by tuning pegs, and the main playing strings can be fine-tuned by sliding a bead threaded on each string just below the bridge.

A black ebony wood Jawari

In one or more of the more common tunings (used by Ravi Shankar, among others, called "Kharaj Pancham" sitar) the playable strings are strung in this fashion:

Chikari strings: Sa (high), Sa (middle), and Pa.

Kharaj (bass) strings: Sa (low) and Pa (low).

Jod and baaj strings, Sa and Ma.

There is a lot of stylistic variance within these tunings, and like most Indian stringed instruments, there is no default tuning. Mostly, tunings vary by schools of teaching (gharana) and the piece that is meant to be played.

flute

flute, French flûte, German Flöte, wind instrument in which the sound is produced by a stream of air directed against a sharp edge, upon which the air breaks up into eddies that alternate regularly above and below the edge, setting into vibration the air enclosed in the flute. In vertical, end-vibrated flutes—such as the Balkan kaval, the Arabic nāy, and panpipes—the player holds the pipe end to his mouth, directing his breath against the opposite edge. In China, South America, Africa, and elsewhere, a notch may be cut in the edge to facilitate sound generation (notched flutes). Vertical nose flutes are also found, especially in Oceania. In transverse, or cross, flutes (i.e., horizontally held and side blown), the stream of breath strikes the opposite rim of a lateral mouth hole. Vertical flutes such as the recorder, in which an internal flue or duct directs the air against a hole cut in the side of the instrument, are known as fipple, or whistle, flutes. Flutes are typically tubular but may also be globular, as with the ocarina and primitive gourd flutes. If a tubular flute is stopped at the lower end, its pitch is an octave lower than that of a comparable open flute.

The earliest example of a Western end-blown flute was discovered in 2008 at Hohle Fels cave near Ulm, Ger. The flute, made from the bone of a griffin vulture, has five finger holes and measures about 8.5 inches (22 cm) long. It is thought to be at least 35,000 years old. Discoveries elsewhere in southwestern Germany yielded other flutes thought to be of similar age.

The characteristic flute of Western music is the transverse flute held sideways to the right of the player. It was known in ancient Greece and Etruria by the 2nd century BCE and was next recorded in India, then China and Japan, where it remains a leading wind instrument. In the 16th century the tenor flute, pitched in G, was played in consort with descant and bass flutes (pitched in D and C respectively). All were typically of boxwood with six finger holes and no keys, semitones being made by cross-fingering (uncovering the holes out of sequence), and retained the cylindrical bore of their Asiatic bamboo relatives. These 16th-century flutes were made obsolete late in the 17th century by the one-keyed conical flute, probably conceived by the celebrated Hotteterre family of makers and players in Paris. A conical flute is made in separate joints, the head joint being cylindrical, the others contracting toward the foot. Two joints were common in the 18th century, the upper being supplied in alternate lengths for tuning purposes. The instrument was known then as the flauto traverso, traversa, or German flute, as distinct from the common flute, usually called the recorder.

From 1760, in order to improve various semitones, three chromatic keys in addition to the original E ♭ key began to be used. By 1800 the typical orchestral flute had these keys plus a lengthened foot joint to C, making six keys altogether. Two more keys produced the eight-keyed flute, which preceded the modern instrument and which lasted, with various auxiliary keys, in some German orchestras into the 20th century.

Theobald Boehm, a Munich flute player and inventor, set out to rationalize the instrument, creating his new conical model in 1832. He replaced the traditional hole layout with an acoustically based one and improved the venting by replacing closed chromatic keys with open-standing keys, devising for their manipulation a system of ring keys on longitudinal axles (rings allow a player to close an out-of-reach key in the same motion as covering a finger hole).

This flute was superseded in 1847 by Boehm's second design, with its experimentally evolved cylindrical bore (having a contracting or parabolic head)—the flute since used. The loss of a certain depth and intimacy of tone of the old conical flute has been offset by gains in evenness of notes, complete expressive control.A modern Boehm-system flute (pitched in C with the range c′–c‴) is made of wood (cocuswood or blackwood) or metal (silver or a substitute). It is 26.5 inches (67 cm) long, with a bore of about 0.75 inch, built in three sections. The body, or middle joint, and the foot joint (sometimes made in one piece) have the note holes (13 at least), which are controlled by an interlocking mechanism of padded key plates hinged on a longitudinal axis. The bore narrows in the head joint, which contains the mouth hole, and is closed just above the hole by a cork or fibre stopper; it is open at the foot end. Other flute sizes include the piccolo, the alto flute (in England sometimes called the bass flute) in G, the bass (or contrabass) flute an octave below the flute, and the various sizes used in military flute bands.

A flute can be described as a woodwind instrument, generally of a tubular shape, that is played by blowing across a specially-shaped opening (known as the embouchure) in such a way as to produce a vibrating column of air whose pulsations we hear as sound. This manner of generating sound by blowing directly across the embouchure distinguishes the flute from other woodwind instruments that produce sound through the use of one or two reeds. The embouchure may be situated either at the end of the tube, as in a recorder, or on the side of the tube, as in the modern flute. A flute whose embouchure is on the side of the tube often is referred to as a "transverse" flute because the player directs the airstream across the side of the tube.

ocarina, (Italian: "little goose",) also called Sweet Potato, globular flute, a late 19th-century musical development of traditional Italian carnival whistles of earthenware, often bird-shaped and sounding only one or two notes. It is an egg-shaped vessel of clay or metal or, as a toy, of plastic and is sounded on the flageolet, or fipple flute, principle. It usually has eight finger holes and two thumbholes and may have a tuning plunger.

In the 1930s it won professional popularity when "sweet potatoes" of different sizes were played in harmony in American popular music. The ocarina is a well-known European example of the globular flute, a form that occurs in many ancient and modern cultures.

The flute is a family of classical music instrument in the woodwind group. Like all woodwinds, flutes are aerophones, meaning they make sound by vibrating a column of air. However, unlike woodwind instruments with reeds, a flute is a reedless wind instrument that produces its sound from the flow of air across an opening. According to the instrument classification of Hornbostel–Sachs, flutes are categorized as edge-blown aerophones. A musician who plays the flute is called a flautist or flutist.

Flutes are the earliest known identifiable musical instruments, as paleolithic examples with hand-bored holes have been found. A number of flutes dating to about 43,000 to 35,000 years ago have been found in the Swabian Jura region of present-day Germany. These flutes demonstrate that a developed musical tradition existed from the earliest period of modern human presence in Europe. While the oldest flutes currently known were found in Europe, Asia, too, has a long history with the instrument that has continued into the present day. In China, a playable bone flute was discovered, dated approximately 9000 years old. The Americas also had an ancient flute culture, with instruments found in Caral, Peru, dating back 5000 years and in Labrador dating back approximately 7500 years.

Historians have found the bamboo flute has a long history as well, especially in China and India. Flutes have been discovered in historical records and artworks starting in the Zhou dynasty. The oldest written sources reveal the Chinese were using the kuan (a reed instrument) and hsio (or xiao, an end-blown flute, often of bamboo) in the 12th–11th centuries BC, followed by the chi (or ch'ih) in the 9th century BC and the yüeh in the 8th century BC.Of these, the chi is the oldest documented cross flute or transverse flute, and was made from bamboo.

The cross flute (Sanskrit: vāṃśī) was "the outstanding wind instrument of ancient India", according to Curt Sachs. He said that religious artwork depicting "celestial music" instruments was linked to music with an "aristocratic character".The Indian bamboo cross flute, Bansuri, was sacred to Krishna, and he is depicted in Hindu art with the instrument.In India, the cross flute appeared in reliefs from the 1st century AD at Sanchi and Amaravati from the 2nd–4th centuries AD.

Although there had been flutes in Europe in prehistoric times, in more recent millennia the flute was absent from the continent until its arrival from Asia, by way of "North Africa, Hungary, and Bohemia", according to historian Alexander Buchner.The end-blown flute began to be seen in illustration in the 11th century. Transverse flutes entered Europe through Byzantium and were depicted in Greek art about 800 AD. The transverse flute had spread into Europe by way of Germany, and was known as the German flute.

The word flute first entered the English language during the Middle English period, as floute, or else flowte, flo(y)te,possibly from Old French flaute and from Old Provençal flaüt, or else from Old French fleüte, flaüte, flahute via Middle High German floite or Dutch fluit. The English verb flout has the same linguistic root, and the modern Dutch verb fluiten still shares the two meanings.Attempts to trace the word back to the Latin flare (to blow, inflate) have been pronounced "phonologically impossible" or "inadmissable".The first known use of the word flute was in the 14th century. According to the Oxford English Dictionary, this was in Geoffrey Chaucer's The Hous of Fame, c.1380.

Today, a musician who plays any instrument in the flute family can be called a flutist or flautist or simply a flute player. Flutist dates back to at least 1603, the earliest quotation cited by the Oxford English Dictionary. Flautist was used in 1860 by Nathaniel Hawthorne in The Marble Faun, after being adopted during the 18th century from Italy (flautista, itself from flauto), like many musical terms in England since the Italian Renaissance. Other English terms, now virtually obsolete, are fluter (15th–19th centuries)and flutenist (17th and 18th centuries)

The oldest flute ever discovered may be a fragment of the femur of a juvenile cave bear, with two to four holes, found at Divje Babe in Slovenia and dated to about 43,000 years ago. However, this has been disputed. In 2008 another flute dated back to at least 35,000 years ago was discovered in Hohle Fels cave near Ulm, Germany.The five-holed flute has a V-shaped mouthpiece and is made from a vulture wing bone. The researchers involved in the discovery officially published their findings in the journal Nature, in August 2009. The discovery was also the oldest confirmed find of any musical instrument in history, until a redating of flutes found in Geißenklösterle cave revealed them to be even older with an age of 42,000 to 43,000 years.

The flute, one of several found, was found in the Hohle Fels cavern next to the Venus of Hohle Fels and a short distance from the oldest known human carving.On announcing the discovery, scientists suggested that the "finds demonstrate the presence of a well-established musical tradition at the time when modern humans colonized Europe".Scientists have also suggested that the discovery of the flute may help to explain "the probable behavioural and cognitive gulf between" Neanderthals and early modern human.

Bone flute made of a goat's tibia, 11th–13th century AD.

A three-holed flute, 18.7 cm long, made from a mammoth tusk (from the Geißenklösterle cave, near Ulm, in the southern German Swabian Alb and dated to 30,000 to 37,000 years ago)was discovered in 2004, and two flutes made from swan bones excavated a decade earlier (from the same cave in Germany, dated to circa 36,000 years ago) are among the oldest known musical instruments.

A playable 9,000-year-old Gudi (literally, "bone flute") was excavated from a tomb in Jiahu along with 29 defunct twins,made from the wing bones of red-crowned cranes with five to eight holes each, in the Central Chinese province of Henan.The earliest extant Chinese transverse flute is a chi (篪) flute discovered in the Tomb of Marquis Yi of Zeng at the Suizhou site, Hubei province, China. It dates from 433 BC, of the later Zhou Dynasty. It is fashioned of lacquered bamboo with closed ends and has five stops that are at the flute's side instead of the top. Chi flutes are mentioned in Shi Jing, compiled and edited by Confucius, according to tradition.

The earliest written reference to a flute is from a Sumerian-language cuneiform tablet dated to c. 2600–2700 BC. Flutes are also mentioned in a recently translated tablet of the Epic of Gilgamesh, an epic poem whose development spanned the period of approximately 2100–600 BC. Additionally, a set of cuneiform tablets knows as the "musical texts" provide precise tuning instructions for seven scale of a stringed instrument (assumed to be a Babylonian lyre). One of those scales is named embūbum, which is an Akkadian word for "flute".

The Bible, in Genesis 4:21, cites Jubal as being the "father of all those who play the ugab and the kinnor". The former Hebrew term is believed by some to refer to some wind instrument, or wind instruments in general, the latter to a stringed instrument, or stringed instruments in general. As such, Jubal is regarded in the Judeo-Christian tradition as the inventor of the flute (a word used in some translations of this biblical passage).Elsewhere in the Bible, the flute is referred to as "chalil" (from the root word for "hollow"), in particular in 1 Samuel 10:5, 1 Kings 1:40, Isaiah 5:12 and 30:29, and Jeremiah 48:36.Archeological digs in the Holy Land have discovered flutes from both the Bronze Age (c. 4000–1200

BC) and the Iron Age (1200–586 BC), the latter era "witness[ing] the creation of the Israelite kingdom and its separation into the two kingdoms of Israel and Judea."

Some early flutes were made out of tibias (shin bones). The flute has also always been an essential part of Indian culture and mythology, and the cross flute believed by several accounts to originate in Indiaas Indian literature from 1500 BC has made vague references to the cross flute.

A flute produces sound when a stream of air directed across a hole in the instrument creates a vibration of air at the hole. The airstream creates a Bernoulli or siphon. This excites the air contained in the usually cylindrical resonant cavity within the flute. The flutist changes the pitch of the sound produced by opening and closing holes in the body of the instrument, thus changing the effective length of the resonator and its corresponding resonant frequency. By varying the air pressure, a flutist can also change the pitch by causing the air in the flute to resonate at a harmonic rather than the fundamental frequency without opening or closing any of the holes.

Head joint geometry appears particularly critical to acoustic performance and tone,but there is no clear consensus on a particular shape amongst manufacturers. Acoustic impedance of the embouchure hole appears the most critical parameter. Critical variables affecting this acoustic impedance include: chimney length (hole between lip-plate and head tube), chimney diameter, and radii or curvature of the ends of the chimney and any designed restriction in the "throat" of the instrument, such as that in the Japanese Nohkan Flute.

A study in which professional flutists were blindfolded could find no significant differences between flutes made from a variety of metals. In two different sets of blind listening, no flute was correctly identified in a first listening, and in a second, only the silver flute was identified. The study concluded that there was "no evidence that the wall material has any appreciable effect on the sound color or dynamic range".

In its most basic form, a flute is an open tube which is blown into. After focused study and training, players use controlled air-direction to create an airstream in which the air is aimed downward into the tone hole of the flute's headjoint. There are several broad classes of flutes. With most flutes, the musician blows directly across the edge of the mouthpiece, with 1/4 of their bottom lip covering the embouchure hole. However, some flutes, such as the whistle, gemshorn, flageolet, recorder, tin whistle, tonette, fujara, and ocarina have a duct that directs the air onto the edge (an arrangement that is termed a "fipple"). These are known as fipple flutes. The fipple gives the instrument a distinct timbre which is different from non-fipple flutes and makes the instrument easier to play, but takes a degree of control away from the musician.

Another division is between side-blown (or transverse) flutes, such as the Western concert flute, piccolo, fife, dizi and bansuri; and end-blown flutes, such as the ney, xiao, kaval, danso, shakuhachi, Anasazi flute and quena. The player of a side-blown flute uses a hole on the side of the tube to produce a tone, instead of blowing on an end of the tube. End-blown flutes should not be confused with fipple flutes such as the recorder, which are also played vertically but have an internal duct to direct the air flow across the edge of the tone hole.

Flutes may be open at one or both ends. The ocarina, xun, pan pipes, police whistle, and bosun's whistle are closed-ended. Open-ended flutes such as the concert flute and the recorder have more harmonics, and thus more flexibility for the player, and brighter timbres. An organ pipe may be either open or closed, depending on the sound desired.

Flutes may have any number of pipes or tubes, though one is the most common number. Flutes with multiple resonators may be played one resonator at a time (as is typical with pan pipes) or more than one at a time (as is typical with double flutes).

Flutes can be played with several different air sources. Conventional flutes are blown with the mouth, although some cultures use nose flutes. The flue pipes of organs, which are acoustically similar to duct flutes, are blown by bellows or fans.

Usually in D, wooden transverse flutes were played in European classical music mainly in the period from the early 18th century to the early 19th century. As such, the instrument is often indicated as baroque flute. Gradually marginalized by the Western concert flute in the 19th century, baroque flutes were again played from the late 20th century as part of the historically informed performance practice.

An illustration of a Western concert flute

The Western concert flute, a descendant of the medieval German flute, is a transverse treble flute that is closed at the top. An embouchure hole is positioned near the top across and into which the flutist blows. The flute has circular tone holes larger than the finger holes of its baroque predecessors. The size and placement of tone holes, key mechanism, and fingering system used to produce the notes in the flute's range were evolved from 1832 to 1847 by Theobald Boehm, who helped greatly improve the instrument's dynamic range and intonation over its predecessors.[48] With some refinements (and the rare exception of the Kingma system and other custom adapted fingering systems), Western concert flutes typically conform to Boehm's design, known as the Boehm system. Beginner's flutes are made of nickel, silver, or brass that is silver-plated, while professionals use solid silver, gold, and sometimes even platinum flutes. There are also modern wooden-bodied flutes usually with silver or gold keywork. The wood is usually African Blackwood.

The standard concert flute is pitched in C and has a range of three octaves starting from middle C or one half step lower when a B foot is attached. This means that the concert flute is one of the highest-pitched common orchestra and concert band instruments.

Center: Piccolo. Right: larger flute

The piccolo plays an octave higher than the regular treble flute. Lower members of the flute family include the G alto and C bass flutes that are used occasionally, and are pitched a perfect fourth and an octave below the concert flute, respectively. The contra-alto, contrabass, subcontrabass, double contrabass, and hyperbass flutes are other rare forms of the flute pitched up to four octaves below middle C.

Other sizes of flutes and piccolos are used from time to time. A rarer instrument of the modern pitching system is the G treble flute. Instruments made according to an older pitch standard, used principally in wind-band music, include D b piccolo, E b soprano flute (Keyed a minor 3rd above the standard C flute), F alto flute, and B b bass flute.

The bamboo flute is an important instrument in Indian classical music, and developed independently of the Western flute. The Hindu God Lord Krishna is traditionally considered a master of the bamboo flute. The Indian flutes are very simple compared to the Western counterparts; they are made of bamboo and are keyless.

Two main varieties of Indian flutes are currently used. The first, the Bansuri (बासुरी), has six finger holes and one embouchure hole, and is used predominantly in the Hindustani music of Northern India. The second, the Venu or Pullanguzhal, has eight finger holes, and is played predominantly in the Carnatic music of Southern India. Presently, the eight-holed flute with cross-fingering technique is common among many Carnatic flutists. Prior to this, the South Indian flute had only seven finger holes, with the fingering standard developed by Sharaba Shastri, of the Palladam school, at the beginning of the 20th century.

Cipriano Garcia playing a flute of the Tohono O'odham culture. Photograph by Frances Densmore taken in 1919.

The quality of the flute's sound depends somewhat on the specific bamboo used to make it, and it is generally agreed that the best bamboo grows in the Nagercoil area of South India.

In 1998 Bharata Natya Shastra Sarana Chatushtai, Avinash Balkrishna Patwardhan developed a methodology to produce perfectly tuned flutes for the ten 'thatas' currently present in Indian Classical Music.

In a regional dialect of Gujarati, a flute is also called Pavo.Some people can also play pair of flutes (Jodiyo Pavo) simultaneously.

CHAPTER SIX

Harmonium

Harmonium is a stringed instrument made of wood, metal, brass, and cloth. A kind of a portable wooden box, it was originated in West Bengal. The harmonium has thus become an integral part of Indian Music. It is extensively used to accompany folk, classical, Sufi, and ghazal compositions for both music and dance.

The keys are played and bellows are compressed simultaneously . When the bellows are compressed, the air passes through the reed, causing it to vibrate. This produces sound. The reed regulates the tone/pitch whereas the bellows produce and control air and the volume. The harmonium can produce up to 12 surs and 22 shrutis.

Harmonium was first designed by Christian Gottlieb Kratzenstein, a professor of physiology at the University of Copenhagen in the 1700s. The design of his harmonium was like a small sized organ. It produced sound with foot-operated bellows which allowed the wind to pass through a pressure-equalizing air reservoir, which allowed the metal reeds (fixed at one end and free at the other) to vibrate. Volume of the instrument was controlled by valves operated by the knee, knobs placed above the keyboard that allowed the wind supply to bypass the reservoir and the force used to pump the bellows. As Europeans emigrated to the United States, they introduced harmonium to the Americans. Eventually the instrument found its way in the colonies of Asia, Africa and Caribbean.

In the early 20th century, usage of harmonium declined in the western world because of people's changing tastes in music. Thus, the European harmonium lost its aura and began to be found only in the museums.

This dying instrument got a second life in India. In 1875, Dwarkanath Ghose designed his version of the Indian hand-pumped harmonium in Calcutta. Traditionally, it was used to accompany the Indian Classical musicians as they used to sit on the floor during performances.

The foot-operated bellows beneath the keyboard in the European harmonium was replaced by the hand-operated bellows at the rear, in the Indian version of harmonium. The new incarnation of the harmonium was more durable, less expensive to build, and easier to maintain and repair. The internal mechanism of the instrument was simplified by Ghose. Drone knobs were added to the instrument to produce harmonies in Indian classical music. A scale changing technique was also added to the Indian version of harmonium. By 1915, India became the leading manufacturer of the harmonium.

The harmonium has thus become an integral part of Indian Music. It is extensively used to accompany folk, classical, sufi and ghazal compositions for both music and dance.

harmonium, also called Reed Organ, free-reed keyboard instrument that produces sound when wind sent by foot-operated bellows through a pressure-equalizing air reservoir causes metal reeds screwed over slots in metal frames to vibrate through the frames with close tolerance. There are no pipes; pitch is determined by the size of the reed. Separate sets of reeds provide different tone colours, the quality of the sound being determined by the characteristic size and shape of the tone chamber surrounding each reed of a given set; constricted chambers, for instance, induce powerful vibration and incisive tone. Volume is controlled by a knee-operated air valve or directly from the bellows pedals by an expression stop that allows the wind supply to bypass the reservoir. The instrument's compass is normally four to five octaves.

The earliest instrument of the harmonium group was the physharmonica, invented in 1818 by Anton Haeckl in Vienna.

His invention was inspired by the Chinese mouth organ, or sheng, which, taken to Russia in the 1770s, had introduced the free reed to Europe and aroused the interest of certain physicists and musicians. Now extinct, other types (such as John Green's seraphine) appeared before Alexandre Debain produced his harmonium in Paris in 1840. The main improvements after 1850 were made by Victor Mustel in Paris and Jacob Estey in the United States.The harmonium was a popular church and household instrument until the electronic organ drove it from the market after the 1930s. Compositions for the instrument include numerous works by the French composers César Franck and Louis Vierne and a quartet for two violins, cello, and harmonium by the Bohemian composer Antonín Dvořák.

Ravanahatha

The ravanahatha (also known as ravanhatta or rawanhattha) is an ancient stringed musical instrument that is suggested to be the precursor to the violin.

It is believed the ravanahatha originated in the Hela civilization of Sri Lanka during the King Ravana reign around 2500 BCE. The instrument was the King's instrument of choice, hence the name, which literally translates as Ravana's hand.The ravanahatha's sound box may be a gourd, a halved coconut shell or hollowed-out cylinder of wood, with a membrane of stretched goat or other hide. A neck of wood or bamboo is attached, carrying between one and four or more peg-tuned strings of gut, hair or steel, strung over a bridge. Some examples may have several sympathetic strings. The bow is usually of horsehair; examples vary in length

In Indian tradition, the ravanahatha is believed to have originated among the Hela people of Lanka during the time of the legendary king Ravana, after whom the instrument is supposedly named. According to legend, Ravana used the ravanahatha in his devotions to the Hindu God Shiva.In the Hindu Ramayana epic, after the war between Rama and Ravana, Hanuman returned to North India with a ravanahatha. The ravanahatha is particularly popular among street musicians in Rajasthan, North India.

Throughout the history of Medieval India, the kings were patrons of music; this helped in increased popularity of the ravanhatha among royal families. In Rajasthan and Gujarat, it was the first musical instrument to be learned by princes. The Sangit tradition of Rajasthan further helped in popularizing ravanhatta among women.[citation needed]

Some sources claim that between the seventh and tenth centuries AD, Arab traders brought the ravanastron from India to the Near East, where it provided the basic model for the Arab rebab, and other early ancestors of the violin family.

Ravanahatha is a primitive string instrument, made up of locally available materials like bamboo, metal pipes and strings, coconut shell, leather, and horse's hair. It is a widely believed fact that Ravanahatha is the precursor for the modern day string instruments like violin.

Evidently, the method of playing a Ravanahatha is quite identical to that of playing a violin. It too includes a bow that is drawn across the strings to create musical vibrations. Furthermore, just like a violin, Ravanahatha has a fingerboard which is used to play the octaves.

The foundational structure of a Ravanahatha includes an 80-90cm long bamboo stem, at the end of which half a coconut shell is attached. To make the shell more vibration-proof, it is covered by goat hide. The stem itself is punctured at regular intervals to fix the knobs which will later help in fine tuning the music. The exclusive part of the instrument is the Bejara (friction reducing powder cake) smoothed hair from horse tail, which makes the sound produced by the instrument unique.

• 55 •

The modern instrument is made up of a bowl-shaped resonator fashioned from a cut coconut shell that is covered with goat hide. The body is the Dandi, a long bamboo stem punctured at regular intervals to fix the knobs which provide the fine-tuning of the ravanahatha. The important part of the instrument is the Bejara – smoothed hair from horsetail, giving the ravanahatha its unique sound. The bow of the instrument often has a bells section which helps the performer to provide rhythm into the melodic pattern.

Panchavadyam

Panchavadyam is the traditional orchestra of Kerala that includes of five different instruments. The instruments are: Timila, Maddalam, Ilathalam, Kombu and idakka. Pachavadyam holds a major position in the temple festivals of the State. In Panchavadyam, Kombu is a wind instrument while the others are percussion instruments. Pachavadyam performance starts with the Timila player. Then all other players except Kombu join him. Kombu player joins at a fixed time.

Panchavadyam (Malayalam: പഞ്ചവാദ്യം), literally meaning an orchestra of five instruments, is basically a temple art form that has evolved in Kerala. Of the five instruments, four — timila, maddalam, ilathalam and idakka — belong to the percussion category, while the fifth, kombu, is a wind instrument.

Much like any chenda melam, panchavadyam is characterised by a pyramid-like rhythmic structure with a constantly increasing tempo coupled with a proportional decrease in the number of beats in cycles. However, in contrast to a chenda melam, panchavadyam uses different instruments (though ilathalam and kompu are common to both), is not related very closely to any temple ritual and, most importantly, permits much personal improvisation while filling up the rhythmic beats on the timila, maddalam and idakka.

Panchavadyam bases itself on the seven-beat thripuda (also spelt thripuda) thaalam (taal) but amusingly sticks to the pattern of the eight-beat chempata thaalam — at least until its last parts. Its pendulum beats in the first stage (pathikaalam) total 896, and halves itself with each stage, making it 448 in the second, 224 in the third, 112 in the fourth and 56 in the fifth. After this, panchavadyam has a relatively loose second half with as many stages, the pendulum beats of which would now scale down to 28, 14, 7, 3.5(three-and-a-half) and 1.

Panchavadyam

Panchavadyam is an orchestra typical of Kerala. It consists of five instruments: kombu, edakka, thimila, ilathalam and maddalam (pancha – five, vadyam - orchestra) Panchavadyam is played during temple festivals like pooram, vela etc.

Thatham Cha Vithatham Chaiva
Ghanam Sushira Meva Cha
Gaanamaananda Nritham Cha
Panchavadya Praveenitha
The four lines define Panchavadyam. The basic rule is to use instruments in the category of thatham, vithatham, ghnanam (non-drum) amd sushiram (wind instrument). Traditionally, five instruments like chenda, kurumkuzhal, thimila, edakka, damanam were played. Besides, it is seen that some texts include veena, venu, mridangam, sanku, padahang also in the definition of Panchavadyam. Today, more than five instruments are played. Edakka, thimila and maddalam are commonly used. In addition to that, sanku and

ilathalam or kombu and ilathalam are used in some places. Thimila, edakka and maddalam are charma instruments; kombu and sanku are sushira instruments, while ilathalam is a ghana instrument. Six different types of music blend together to create musical delight, ie. Panchavadyam.

In Panchavadyam there is no limit to the number of performers. But there are certain calculations as to the number of instruments to be played. The number of thimila is double that of maddalam plus one more, while kombu equals the number of thimila, the same number of ilathalam is required. For a short Panchavadyam, one edakka may be played. For a large Panchavadyam, two edakkas are played. However, one sanku (conch) would do. In rare cases one may see many conchs being blown.

The thimila artiste and the maddalam artiste stand face to face while presenting Panchavadyam. The expert or leader among the thimila players stands in the middle. Likewise, the maddalam expert. Ilathalam artistes stand behind the thimila artistes. The kombu artistes stand behind the maddalam players. The sanku (conch) blowers position on the right hand side of the edakka players who are on the right side. This is a traditional rule. But these positions change when Panchavadyam is performed on stage or in a procession. It is also not rare to see all of them performing in a row.

It is assumed that this art form originated in today's Eranakulam. There were a lot of thimila artistes in places like Ramamangalam, Perumballi, Keezhilam, Chottanikkara, Cheranellur, Kaladi, Nayathodu, Chengamanad. Later, it extended to Thrissur and Palakkad districts.
In the 1920s maddalam vidwan Thiruvilwamala Venkiteswar Iyer (Venkitachan Swamy), Panchavadya expert Annamada Achutha Marar, thimila vidwan Chengamanad vidwan

Sekhara Kurup made attempts at refining and improving the art form. In the period 1920-1930, Venkitachan Swamy coming to the Thrissur pooram madom had the maddalam tied to his waist (in the past the maddalam was played hanging it on one's neck). This was a shocking sight to the onlookers. Though there was a lot of opposition, it was later accepted. With many individuals taking interest, Panchavadyam no longer was confined to temples and it attained a unique status as a form of distinct art.

Whether panchavadyam is originally a feudal art is still a matter of debate among scholars, but its elaborate form in vogue today came into existence in the 1930s. It was primarily the brainchild of late maddalam artistes Venkichan Swami (Thiruvillwamala Venkateswara Iyer) and his disciple Madhava Warrier in association with late timila masters Annamanada Achutha Marar and Chengamanad Sekhara Kurup. Subsequently it was promoted the late idakka master Pattirath Sankara Marar. They dug space for a stronger foundation (the Pathikaalam), thus making pachavadyam a five-stage (kaalam) concert with an intelligent mixture of composed and improvised parts. Spanning about two hours, it has several phrases where each set of the instruments complement the others more like harmony in the Western orchestra than the concept of melody in India. Much like in Panchari and other kinds of chenda melam, panchavadyam, too, has its artistes lined up in two oval-shaped halves, facing each other. However, unlike any classical chenda melam, panchavadyam seemingly gains pace in the early stages itself, thereby tending to sound more casual and breezy right from its start, beginning after three lengthy, stylised blows on the conch (shankhu).

A panchavadyam is anchored and led by the timila artist at the centre of his band of instrumentalists, behind whom line up the ilathalam players. Opposite them stand the maddalam players in a row, and behind them are the kompu players. Idakka players, usually two, stand on both sides of the aisle separating the timila and maddalam line-up. A major panchavadyam will have 60 artistes.

Ghatam

The ghatam is an ancient Indian percussion instrument that plays a large part in South Indian Carnatic classical music tradition. Other names for this instrument include bada, ghara, matka, and noot. The ghatam is considered an idiophone because the whole of it vibrates to produce a sound when struck—unlike membranophones which have drum heads that are struck, like the tabla or mridangam.

The ghatam instrument itself is a rounded, earthenware pot with a narrow opening at the top. The mouth of the pot has an outer rim above a narrow neck. The body, neck, and rim of the instrument each produce a different tone when struck. The ghatam is known for its deep, sometimes metallic sound in various pitches and often accompanies the mridangam in concert performances or percussion ensembles.

Although the ghatam looks like a regular clay pot, it is specially made to be an instrument. The instrument comes in many different sizes and is made from a mixture of clay, mud, and sometimes metals (typically brass or copper). The thickness of the pot must be even to produce a quality tone. Ghatams are made in many places in India but most famous are those made in Manamadurai, which produces ghatams that are thicker and heavier with a distinct sound.

The ghatam is played with the fingers and palms of both hands—producing fast, complex Carnatic rhythms. Ghatam music provides the 'heartbeat' for many of the pieces it accompanies. The instrument is positioned either on the lap of the seated player or in front of them on a chutta or bira, the ring-shaped cloth base for tabla. In South Indian technique, the opening is pressed against the player's stomach.

Although there are many clay pots that have been used as instruments all over the world throughout history, none have maintained the popularity and sophistication of the ghatam. Ghatam meaning comes from the word ghata in Sanskrit, meaning pot. The ghatam as an instrument was first described by Sage Valmiki in the ancient poem Ramayana, dated roughly 500 CE. The sound the ghatam makes when played has been described in several other Sanskrit texts on rhythm and music, including the Tamil text Silappatikaram from around the same period of time. It is thought that the first ghatams may have had skins covering the opening, making them an idiophone and a membranophone, but since the folk music practices of the 6th century to now, the ghatam has not had a membrane stretched across the mouth of the instrument.

The ghatam began as a folk instrument in several parts of India and remains a prominent part of many folk traditions today, particularly in Punjab. It wasn't until the 19th century that the ghatam was included in South Indian Carnatic classical music performances. In the 1800s, Polagam Chidambara Iyer was said to have been the first concert ghatam vidvan (a master of one's art), introducing the folk instrument to Carnatic concerts. Years later, Palani Krishna Iyer is said to have developed rhythm patterns and playing techniques specific to the ghatam. However, tabla techniques are still used by some contemporary ghatam players.

In Carnatic music, the ghatam is considered an additional, or secondary, instrument that is meant to back up the mridangam. However, over the last 50 to 100 years the ghatam has gained increasing popularity, becoming a more prominent solo instrument, as well. In addition to traditional and classical Indian music, the ghatam is finding popularity abroad. In the last few decades, this unique percussion instrument has become prominent in many world fusion genres, as well as rock and jazz music.

Types of Ghatam Musical Instrument

Ghatam musical instrument used in South Indian Carnatic classical music has some minor differences because of the different makers but are mostly similar. They come in many different sizes but have the same colouring and dimensions to maintain the quality of sound. The red/orange colour of the ghatam is due to the clay, metals and glazing process.

Most South Indian ghatams for Carnatic music are made in either Chennai or Manamadurai. Those made in Chennai are called Madras ghatam and are typically thinner than the Manamadurai ghatam because they are made from only clay. Madras Ghatams are considered easier to play than their much heavier counterparts. For this reason, the Madras ghatam is recommended for students who are just starting out learning ghatam music. Manamadurai Ghatams are made with brass or copper pieces, creating a very distinct, deep, metallic sound.

The North Indian version of the ghatam, called the ghara, is very similar but has thinner walls and is blue/gray in color due to graphite being used in the construction, along with clay and other metals. These are heavier than Madras ghatams but lighter than Manamadurai ghatams. Gharas are typically played with mallets instead of the player's hands.

The matka is the version of ghatam popular in Gujarat and Jaipur. Unlike other ghatams, the matka doubles as a cooking or storage vessel when not being used as an instrument. Players of this type of ghatam may wear metal rings on certain fingers to produce sharper, staccato sounds.

Playing Techniques

Playing style varies by location and teacher. In Carnatic classical music, where the techniques are more standardized, the instrument is played with the mouth of the pot pressed against the stomach. Changing the pressure of the pot against the stomach changes the resonance and pitch of the sound. In other styles, such as North Indian tradition, the pot is typically played upright.

South Indian Ghatam players use the hand positions that are typical of other percussion instruments to produce the complex rhythms that Indian percussion style is known for. While the ghatam has specific positions for playing, it also borrows from mridangam and tabla hand positions. The body, neck, and rim are played with multiple fingers, palm, and wrist positions but the ghatam makes another unique sound, as well. When the mouth of the pot is struck with the palm, it creates a low resonate sound.

The ghatam is also a very popular instrument for improvisation and movement—to the delight of many audiences. The ghatam is the only instrument that changes position while being played, as the musician may change the direction of the instrument to achieve a different pitch or tone. Some ghatam vidvans even throw the pot in the air and catch it while maintaining the rhythm to entertain audiences. It is said that ghatam players were the jesters of early Carnatic performances.

Ghatam Mechanics

Each ghatam has a singular pitch of its own because it depends on the size, thickness, and temperature the pot is fired at. The larger and heavier the pot is, the lower the pitch is—while smaller pots have a higher pitch. The pitch can be altered slightly by applying water or clay putty to the inside of the pot but this practice is not exact and requires repeating to maintain the difference. For this reason, a professional ghatam player may have several different sizes for a single performance.

The ghatam has three main playing areas, the upper, middle, and bottom portions, each of which has their own distinct sections. When a student takes ghatam lessons, they learn how to speak and then play the different notes (called konnakol in Carnatic classical music and bols in Hindustani classical music) and where to play them to achieve the desired sound.ghatam, large, narrow-mouthed earthenware water pot used as a percussion instrument in India.

Unlike other Indian percussion instruments, such as the tabla and mridangam, the ghatam does not have a membrane over its mouth. Ghatam produce a distinctive metallic sound and are made in several sizes, each size having a different pitch. As used in Karnatak music, the ghatam is positioned with its mouth pressed against the player's stomach. The player taps the surface of the ghatam with the fingers and the base of the palm and changes the pitch and resonance of the instrument by varying the pressure of the pot against the stomach. The ghatam is usually found in folk music, but it has also become popular in classical music genres. In Kashmir the instrument is known as a noot and is placed in an upright position for playing.

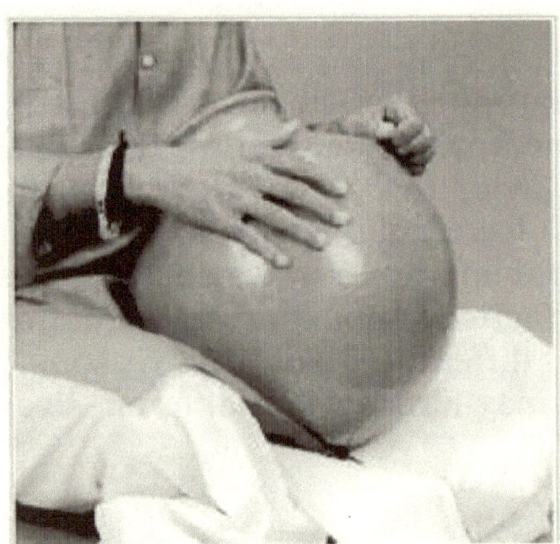

Drum

drum, musical instrument, the sound of which is produced by the vibration of a stretched membrane (it is thus classified as a membranophone within the larger category of percussion instruments). Basically, a drum is either a tube or a bowl of wood, metal, or pottery (the "shell") covered at one or both ends by a membrane (the "head"), which is usually struck by a hand or stick. Friction drums, a class apart, are sounded by rubbing.

Drums appear with wide geographic distribution in archaeological excavations from Neolithic times onward; one excavated in Moravia is dated to 6000 BCE. Early drums consisted of a section of hollowed tree trunk covered at one end with reptile or fish skin and were struck with the hands. Later the skin was taken from hunted game or cattle, and sticks were used. The double-headed drum came later, as did pottery drums in various shapes. The heads were fastened by several methods, some still in use. The skin might be secured to single-headed drums by pegs, nails, glue, buttoning (through holes in the membrane), or neck lacing (wrapping a cord around the membrane overlap). Double-headed drums were often directly cord-tensioned (i.e., through holes in the skin). Modern European orchestral drums often combine two hoops pressing against each head (one rolled in the skin, the other outside) with indirect lacing (i.e., to the hoops).

Drums typically have conspicuous extramusical functions—civil, message transmitting, and, particularly, religious. Credited with magical powers, they are frequently held sacred. In many societies their manufacture involves ritual. In East Africa, offerings such as cattle are made to the royal kettledrums, which not only symbolize the king's power and status but also offer him supernatural protection.

Frame drums were played in the ancient Middle East (chiefly by women), Greece, and Rome and reached medieval Europe through Islamic culture. Their shape varies (round, octagonal, square, etc.), they may have one or two heads, and they may have attached jingles or snares. Possibly of different origin are the frame drums used in the magico-religious ceremonies of shamans (a priest or priestess who uses magic for the purpose of curing the sick, divining the hidden, and controlling events) in Central Asia, the Arctic regions, and North America. Double-headed frame drums with enclosed pellets (found in India and Tibet Autonomous Region of China) are known as rattle drums.

Shallow kettledrums are first depicted about 600 CE in Persia. Larger kettledrums, mentioned with the smaller type in the 10th century, are not pictured alone until the 12th. Though originally of clay and cord braced, kettledrums were later made of metal (or sometimes wood). They spread with Islamic culture through Europe, Africa, and Asia.

Little is known about medieval European drums and drumming, the only evidence being pictures and written references; no medieval drums survive. Written percussion parts (in instruction books only) date from the 16th century, as drummers were expected to extemporize their parts. By the 13th century three types of drum appear to have been established: the nakers, small paired kettledrums; the tab, a small cylindrical drum, often with snares; and the tambourine. They apparently served only as time beaters and, except for the tambourine, were beaten with sticks. Only from about the 14th century were drums built to produce loud, carrying sounds, a result of the introduction of mercenary infantry troops, in whose regiments fifes were soon paired with drums. Large kettledrums were associated with royalty and nobility. They entered the orchestra as a purely musical instrument in the mid-17th century, the bass drum (derived from the long drums of Turkish Janissary troops; see Janissary music) during the 18th century, and the military-derived snare drum (side drum) during the 19th.

Drums figure prominently in the 21st century in numerous musical genres around the world.

Frame drums were played in the ancient Middle East (chiefly by women), Greece, and Rome and reached medieval Europe through Islamic culture. Their shape varies (round, octagonal, square, etc.), they may have one or two heads, and they may have attached jingles or snares. Possibly of different origin are the frame drums used in the magico-religious ceremonies of shamans (a priest or priestess who uses magic for the purpose of curing the sick, divining the hidden, and controlling events) in Central Asia, the Arctic regions, and North America. Double-headed frame drums with enclosed pellets (found in India and Tibet Autonomous Region of China) are known as rattle drums.

Shallow kettledrums are first depicted about 600 CE in Persia. Larger kettledrums, mentioned with the smaller type in the 10th century, are not pictured alone until the 12th. Though originally of clay and cord braced, kettledrums were later made of metal (or sometimes wood). They spread with Islamic culture through Europe, Africa, and Asia.

Little is known about medieval European drums and drumming, the only evidence being pictures and written references; no medieval drums survive. Written percussion parts (in instruction books only) date from the 16th century, as drummers were expected to extemporize their parts. By the 13th century three types of drum appear to have been established: the nakers, small paired kettledrums; the tab, a small cylindrical drum, often with snares; and the tambourine. They apparently served only as time beaters and, except for the tambourine, were beaten with sticks. Only from about the 14th century were drums built to produce loud, carrying sounds, a result of the introduction of mercenary infantry troops, in whose regiments fifes were soon paired with drums. Large kettledrums were associated with royalty and nobility. They entered the orchestra as a purely musical instrument in the mid-17th century, the bass drum (derived from the long drums of Turkish Janissary troops; see Janissary music) during the 18th century, and the military-derived snare drum (side drum) during the 19th.

Drums figure prominently in the 21st century in numerous musical genres around the world.

Drums are usually played by striking with the hand, a beater attached to a pedal, or with one or two sticks with or without padding. A wide variety of sticks are used, including wooden sticks and sticks with soft beaters of felt on the end. In jazz, some drummers use brushes for a smoother, quieter sound. In many traditional cultures, drums have a symbolic function and are used in religious ceremonies. Drums are often used in music therapy, especially hand drums, because of their tactile nature and easy use by a wide variety of people

In popular music and jazz, "drums" usually refers to a drum kit or a set of drums (with some cymbals, or in the case of harder rock music genres, many cymbals), and "drummer" to the person who plays them.

Drums acquired even divine status in places such as Burundi, where the karyenda was a symbol of the power of the king.

The shell almost always has a circular opening over which the drumhead is stretched, but the shape of the remainder of the shell varies widely. In the Western musical tradition, the most usual shape is a cylinder, although timpani, for example, use bowl-shaped shells.[1] Other shapes include a frame design (tar, Bodhrán), truncated cones (bongo drums, Ashiko), goblet shaped (djembe), and joined truncated cones (talking drum).

Drums with cylindrical shells can be open at one end (as is the case with timbales), or can have two drum heads, one head on each end. Single-headed drums typically consist of a skin stretched over an enclosed space, or over one of the ends of a hollow vessel. Drums with two heads covering both ends of a cylindrical shell often have a small hole somewhat halfway between the two heads; the shell forms a resonating chamber for the resulting sound. Exceptions include the African slit drum, also known as a log drum as it is made from a hollowed-out tree trunk, and the Caribbean steel drum, made from a metal barrel. Drums with two heads can also have a set of wires, called snares, held across the bottom head, top head, or both heads, hence the name snare drum.[1] On some drums with two heads, a hole or bass reflex port may be cut or installed onto one head, as with some 2010s era bass drums in rock music.

On modern band and orchestral drums, the drumhead is placed over the opening of the drum, which in turn is held onto the shell by a "counterhoop" (or "rim"), which is then held by means of a number of tuning screws called "tension rods" that screw into lugs placed evenly around the circumference. The head's tension can be adjusted by loosening or tightening the rods. Many such drums have six to ten tension rods. The sound of a drum depends on many variables—including shape, shell size and thickness, shell materials, counterhoop material, drumhead material, drumhead tension, drum position, location, and striking velocity and angle.

Prior to the invention of tension rods, drum skins were attached and tuned by rope systems—as on the Djembe—or pegs and ropes such as on Ewe drums. These methods are rarely used today, though sometimes appear on regimental marching band snare drums. The head of a talking drum, for example, can be temporarily tightened by squeezing the ropes that connect the top and bottom heads. Similarly, the tabla is tuned by hammering a disc held in place around the drum by ropes stretching from the top to bottom head. Orchestral timpani can be quickly tuned to precise pitches by using a foot pedal.

Several factors determine the sound a drum produces, including the type, shape and construction of the drum shell, the type of drum heads it has, and the tension of these drumheads. Different drum sounds have different uses in music. For example, the modern Tom-tom drum. A jazz drummer may want drums that are high pitched, resonant and quiet whereas a rock drummer may prefer drums that are loud, dry and low-pitched.

The drum head has the most effect on how a drum sounds. Each type of drum head serves its own musical purpose and has its own unique sound. Double-ply drumheads dampen high frequency harmonics because they are heavier and they are suited to heavy playing. Drum heads with a white, textured coating on them muffle the overtones of the drum head slightly, producing a less diverse pitch. Drum heads with central silver or black dots tend to muffle the overtones even more, while drum heads with perimeter sound rings mostly eliminate overtones. Some jazz drummers avoid using thick drum heads, preferring single ply drum heads or drum heads with no muffling. Rock drummers often prefer the thicker or coated drum heads.

The second biggest factor that affects drum sound is head tension against the shell. When the hoop is placed around the drum head and shell and tightened down with tension rods, the tension of the head can be adjusted. When the tension is increased, the amplitude of the sound is reduced and the frequency is increased, making the pitch higher and the volume lower.

The type of shell also affects the sound of a drum. Because the vibrations resonate in the shell of the drum, the shell can be used to increase the volume and to manipulate the type of sound produced. The larger the diameter of the shell, the lower the pitch. The larger the depth of the drum, the louder the volume. Shell thickness also determines the volume of drums. Thicker shells produce louder drums. Mahogany raises the frequency of low pitches and keeps higher frequencies at about the same speed. When choosing a set of shells, a jazz drummer may want smaller maple shells, while a rock drummer may want larger birch shells.

CHAPTER ELEVEN

Guitar

The guitar is a string instrument which is played by plucking the strings. The main parts of a guitar are the body, the fretboard, the headstock and the strings. Guitars are usually made from wood or plastic. Their strings are made of steel or nylon.

The guitar strings are plucked with the fingers and fingernails of the right hand (or left hand, for left handed players), or a small pick made of thin plastic. This type of pick is called a "plectrum" or guitar pick. The left hand holds the neck of the guitar while the fingers pluck the strings. Different finger positions on the fretboard make different notes.

Guitar-like plucked string instruments have been used for many years. In many countries and at many different time periods, guitars and other plucked string instruments have been very popular, because they are light to carry from place to place, they are easier to learn to play than many other instruments. Guitars are used for many types of music, from Classical to Rock. Most pieces of popular music that have been written since the 1950s are written with guitars.

There are many different types of guitars, classified on how they are made and the type of music they are used for. All traditional types of guitar have a body which is hollow. This makes the sound of the strings louder, and gives the guitar its quality. This type of guitar is called "acoustic". (An acoustic instrument is one that makes its own dynamics.)

From the 1930s, people started making and playing guitars that used electricity and amplifiers to control the loudness. These guitars, which are often used in popular music, are called electric guitars. They do not need to have a hollow body. This is because they do not use acoustics to amplify the sound.

Most guitars have six strings, but there are also guitars with four, seven, eight, ten, or twelve strings. More strings make the instrument sound fuller. The neck of a guitar has bars or marks called frets. Frets help a guitarist know where to put his or her fingers to get the right pitch when playing. Standard tuning defines the string pitches as E, A, D, G, B, and E, from lowest (low E2) to highest (high E4). Standard tuning is used by most guitarists, and frequently used tunings can be understood as variations on standard tuning.

The word guitar was adopted into English from Spanish word guitarra in the 1600s. In the Middle Ages the word gitter or gittern was used in England. Both guitarra and gitter came from the Latin word cithara. The word cithara came from the earlier Greek word kithara. Kithara could have come from the Persian word sehtār[source?]. seh meaning "three" and tār meaning "string". There is also a similar but two-stringed Persian instrument named dotār. do means "two" in Persian. The Indian sitar instrument was named after the Persian sehtār.The sihtar itself is related to the Indian instrument, the sitar.

A person who plays a guitar is called a guitarist. A person who makes or fixes guitars is a luthier, which comes from the word "lute". The word "lute", comes from the Arabic "Al-Uud", a stringed instrument from the Middle East. The guitar appears to be derived from earlier instruments known in ancient central Asia as the Sitara. Instruments very similar to the guitar appear in ancient carvings and statues recovered from the old Iranian capitol of Susa. The modern word, guitar, was adopted into English from the Spanish word guitarra, which came from the older Greek word kithara. Possible sources for various names of musical instruments that guitar could be derived from appear to be a combination of two Indo-European roots[source?]: guit-, similar to Sanskrit sangeet meaning "music", and -tar a widely found root meaning "cord" or "string". The word guitar is a word that the Iberian Arabic language took from the Persian language. The word qitara is an Arabic name for various members of the lute family that preceded the Western guitar. The word guitarra was introduced into Spanish when such instruments were brought into Iberia by the Moors after the 10th century.

There have been instruments like the guitar for at least 5,000 years. The guitar may have come from older instruments known as the sitara from ancient India and central Asia. The oldest known picture of a guitar-like instrument is a 3300 year old stone carving of a Hittite bard. The oldest guitar-like instrument that is still complete is the "Warwick Gittern" in the British Museum. It belonged to Elizabeth I of England and probably to her father Henry VIII before it was given to her.[3] It is about 500 years old.

The design of the modern guitar began with the Roman cithara. The cithara was brought by the Romans to Hispania (Spain) around 40 AD. In the 8th century the Moors brought the four-stringed oud into Spain. The introduction to the oud caused changes to the design of the cithara.In other parts of Europe, the six-string Scandinavian lut (lute) became popular wherever the Vikings had been. By 1200 AD, there were two types of the four string "guitar": the guitarra morisca (Moorish guitar) from Spain which had a rounded back, wide fingerboard and several soundholes, and the guitarra latina (Latin guitar) which was more like the modern guitar with one sound hole and a narrower neck.

The Spanish vihuela, of the 16th century, was another instrument similar to the guitar. It had lute-style tuning and a body that was like a guitar. The vihuela was only popular for a short amount of time. It is not known whether it was simply a design that combined features of the oud and lute or a transition from the Renaissance instrument to the modern guitar.

The Vinaccia family from Naples, Italy were famous mandolin makers. It is thought that they also made the oldest six-string guitar that still exists. There is a guitar built that was signed and dated 1779 on the label by Gaetano Vinaccia (1759 - after 1831) Although there are many fakes that have dates on them from that time, this guitar is believed by experts to be genuine (real).

The guitar's design was improved (made better) by the famous Spanish luthier, Antonio Torres Jurado (1817-1892) and by Louis Panormo of London.

The electric guitar was made by George Beauchamp in 1936. Beauchamp co-founded a company called Rickenbacher to make guitars. However, Danelectro was the first to produce electric guitars for the public to use.

CHAPTER TWELVE

Piano

The piano is an acoustic, keyboard and stringed musical instrument in which the strings are struck by wooden hammers that are coated with a softer material (modern hammers are covered with dense wool felt; some early pianos used leather). It is played using a keyboard, which is a row of keys (small levers) that the performer presses down or strikes with the fingers and thumbs of both hands to cause the hammers to strike the strings. It was invented in Italy by Bartolomeo Cristofori around the year 1700 (the exact year is uncertain).

The piano has been an extremely popular instrument in Western classical music since the late 18th century. The piano was invented by Bartolomeo Cristofori of Padua, Italy. He made his first piano in 1709. It developed from the clavichord which looks like a piano but the strings of a clavichord are hit by a small blade of metal called a "tangent".[1] In the piano the strings are hit by a block of wood called a hammer. The early keyboarded instruments, such as the clavichords, harpsichords and organs that were used at that time, had a much shorter keyboard than they do today. Gradually the keyboard became longer until it had the 88 notes (7 octaves plus three notes) of the modern piano.

At first the instrument was called the "fortepiano". This means "loud-soft" in Italian. It was given this name because it could be played either loudly or softly, depending on how hard the note was hit (the harpsichord could not do this, and the clavichord could only make a tiny difference between louder and softer). Later this name changed to "pianoforte". This is normally shortened to "piano". The word "fortepiano" is sometimes used to describe the pianos of the late 18th and early 19th centuries. In some languages, such as Russian, "fortepiano" is the normal word for a piano.

Although the piano was invented at the beginning of the 18th century, it was not until 50 years later that it started to become popular. The first time the piano was played in a public concert in London was in 1768 when it was played by Johann Christian Bach The upright piano was invented in 1800 by John Isaac Hawkings. Seven years later T. Southwell invented "over-stringing". This means that the strings for the low notes go diagonally across the soundboard so that they can be longer and make a much bigger sound.

The early pianos had strings that were fastened to a frame made of wood. They were not very heavy, but they were not very strong or loud, so they could not be heard very well in a big concert hall. In 1825 the cast-iron frame was invented in America. This made the piano much stronger so that it could make a bigger sound and the strings were not likely to break.

One of the most known fortepiano builders was Johann Andreas Stein from Augsburg, Germany. Stein developed the "Viennese" action, popular on Viennese pianos up to the mid-19th century. Another important Viennese piano maker was Anton Walter.Mozart's own Walter fortepiano is presently at the Mozart Museum in Salzburg, Austria. Haydn also owned Walter piano, and Beethoven expressed a wish to buy one. The most famous early-romantic piano maker was Conrad Graf (1782–1851), who made Beethoven's last piano.His instrumentsplayed by Chopin, Mendelssohn and Schumann. Johannes Brahms had preferred pianos by Johann Baptist Streicher.[8] The English piano school builders included Johannes Zumpe, Robert Stodart and John Broodwood. Prominent piano makers among the French during the era of the fortepiano included Erard, Pleyel (Chopin's favorite maker) and Boisselot (Liszt's favorite)

At the bottom of every modern piano, there are at least two pedals, which are levers that the pianist presses down with his or her feet to change the sound. Many pianos have three pedals, but a few have even more. Each pedal changes the sound in a different way.

The three pedals of a piano. From left to right, they are the soft, sostenuto, and sustain (damper) pedals.

The damper pedal (also called the sustain pedal) is the pedal on the right, and the one that is used most often. For this reason, it is often called just "the pedal". It is pressed with the pianist's right foot, and makes the dampers (which look a bit like the hammers) that usually rests on the strings come off, so the strings are free to vibrate. As long as the pianist holds this pedal down, the notes he plays will keep on sounding even when he takes his fingers off the keys. Some other strings will also vibrate very lightly (this is called "sympathetic vibration"), which makes the sound smoother and richer. Pianists have to learn how to use this pedal well. This will depend on such things as the style of the music, the size of the piano, the size and the acoustics of the room in which the instrument is in.

The soft pedal (also called the una corda pedal) is the pedal on the left, and is pressed with the pianist's left foot. As its name suggests, this pedal makes the notes sound quieter. On a grand piano, the whole keyboard and action shift a bit to the left so that the hammers only hit two strings instead of three. The soft pedal is usually used only in classical music and is normally kept down for the whole of a piece or a section of a piece.

On pianos with three pedals, the pedal in the middle does different things on a grand and upright piano. On a grand piano, it is the sostenuto pedal, and is pressed with the pianist's left foot. Like the right pedal, it keeps the sound going, but only on the notes that are being played at the moment when the middle pedal is pressed down. This makes it possible to keep one chord going while playing other notes that will not carry on. All concert grand pianos have a sostenuto pedal, and some modern upright pianos do as well. The middle pedal on some upright pianos is not a sostenuto pedal at all, but a practice pedal. It places a piece of cloth in front of the strings, making the sound very quiet so that a pianist can practice without disturbing other people. The practice pedal can usually be pressed down and put in a slot so that it will stay in place.

CHAPTER THIRTEEN

Violin

The violin, sometimes known as a fiddle, is a wooden chordophone (string instrument) in the violin family. Most violins have a hollow wooden body. It is the smallest and thus highest-pitched instrument (soprano) in the family in regular use. The violin typically has four strings (some can have five), usually tuned in perfect fifths with notes G3, D4, A4, E5, and is most commonly played by drawing a bow across its strings. It can also be played by plucking the strings with the fingers (pizzicato) and, in specialized cases, by striking the strings with the wooden side of the bow (col legno).

Violins are important instruments in a wide variety of musical genres. They are most prominent in the Western classical tradition, both in ensembles (from chamber music to orchestras) and as solo instruments. Violins are also important in many varieties of folk music, including country music, bluegrass music, and in jazz. Electric violins with solid bodies and piezoelectric pickups are used in some forms of rock music and jazz fusion, with the pickups plugged into instrument amplifiers and speakers to produce sound. The violin has come to be incorporated in many non-Western music cultures, including Indian music and Iranian music. The name fiddle is often used regardless of the type of music played on it.

The violin was first known in 16th-century Italy, with some further modifications occurring in the 18th and 19th centuries to give the instrument a more powerful sound and projection. In Europe, it served as the basis for the development of other stringed instruments used in Western classical music, such as the violine.

Violinists and collectors particularly prize the fine historical instruments made by the Stradivari, Guarneri, Guadagnini and Amati families from the 16th to the 18th century in Brescia and Cremona (Italy) and by Jacob Stainer in Austria. According to their reputation, the quality of their sound has defied attempts to explain or equal it, though this belief is disputed.Great numbers of instruments have come from the hands of less famous makers, as well as still greater numbers of mass-produced commercial "trade violins" coming from cottage industries in places such as Saxony, Bohemia, and Mirecourt. Many of these trade instruments were formerly sold by Sears, Roebuck and Co. and other mass merchandisers.

The components of a violin are usually made from different types of wood. Violins can be strung with gut, Perlon or other synthetic, or steel strings. A person who makes or repairs violins is called a luthier or violinmaker. One who makes or repairs bows is called an archetier or bowmaker.

The earliest stringed instruments were mostly plucked (for example, the Greek lyre). Two-stringed, bowed instruments, played upright and strung and bowed with horsehair, may have originated in the nomadic equestrian cultures of Central Asia, in forms closely resembling the modern-day Mongolian Morin huur and the Kazakh Kobyz. Similar and variant types were probably disseminated along east–west trading routes from Asia into the Middle East,and the

Byzantine Empire

The origin of the violin family is obscure.Some say that the bow was introduced to Europe from the Middle East while others say the bow was not introduced from the Middle East but the other way round and that that the bow may have had its origin from a more frequent intercourse with North Europe and Western EuropeThe first makers of violins probably borrowed from various developments of the Byzantine lyra. These included the vielle (also known as the fidel or viuola) and the lira da braccio. The violin in its present form emerged in early 16th-century northern Italy. The earliest pictures of violins, albeit with three strings, are seen in northern Italy around 1530, at around the same time as the words "violino" and "vyollon" are seen in Italian and French documents. One of the earliest explicit descriptions of the instrument, including its tuning, is from the Epitome musical by Jambe de Fer, published in Lyon in 1556. By this time, the violin had already begun to spread throughout Europe.

The violin proved very popular, both among street musicians and the nobility; the French king Charles IX ordered Andrea Amati to construct 24 violins for him in 1560.One of these "noble" instruments, the Charles IX, is the oldest surviving violin. The finest Renaissance carved and decorated violin in the world is the Gasparo da Salò (c.1574) owned by Ferdinand II, Archduke of Austria and later, from 1841, by the Norwegian virtuoso Ole Bull, who used it for forty years and thousands of concerts, for its very powerful and beautiful tone, similar to that of a Guarneri."The Messiah" or "Le Messie" (also known as the "Salabue") made by Antonio Stradivari in 1716 remains pristine. It is now located in the Ashmolean Museum of Oxford

A violin generally consists of a spruce top (the soundboard, also known as the top plate, table, or belly), maple ribs and back, two endblocks, a neck, a bridge, a soundpost, four strings, and various fittings, optionally including a chinrest, which may attach directly over, or to the left of, the tailpiece. A distinctive feature of a violin body is its hourglass-like shape and the arching of its top and back. The hourglass shape comprises two upper bouts, two lower bouts, and two concave C-bouts at the waist, providing clearance for the bow. The "voice" or sound of a violin depends on its shape, the wood it is made from, the graduation (the thickness profile) of both the top and back, the varnish that coats its outside surface and the skill of the luthier in doing all of these steps. The varnish and especially the wood continue to improve with age, making the fixed supply of old well-made violins built by famous luthiers much sought-after.

The majority of glued joints in the instrument use animal hide glue rather than common white glue for a number of reasons. Hide glue is capable of making a thinner joint than most other glues. It is reversible (brittle enough to crack with carefully applied force and removable with hot water) when disassembly is needed. Since fresh hide glue sticks to old hide glue, more original wood can be preserved when repairing a joint. (More modern glues must be cleaned off entirely for the new joint to be sound, which generally involves scraping off some wood along with the old glue.) Weaker, diluted glue is usually used to fasten the top to the ribs, and the nut to the fingerboard, since common repairs involve removing these parts. The purfling running around the edge of the spruce top provides some protection against cracks originating at the edge. It also allows the top to flex more independently of the rib structure. Painted-on faux purfling on the top is usually a sign of an inferior instrument. The back and ribs are typically made of maple, most often with a matching striped figure, referred to as flame, fiddleback, or tiger stripe.

The neck is usually maple with a flamed figure compatible with that of the ribs and back. It carries the fingerboard, typically made of ebony, but often some other wood stained or painted black on cheaper instruments. Ebony is the preferred material because of its hardness, beauty, and superior resistance to wear. Fingerboards are dressed to a particular transverse curve, and have a small lengthwise "scoop," or concavity, slightly more pronounced on the lower strings, especially when meant for gut or synthetic strings. Some old violins (and some made to appear old) have a grafted scroll, evidenced by a glue joint between the pegbox and neck. Many authentic old instruments have had their necks reset to a slightly increased angle, and lengthened by about a centimeter. The neck graft allows the original scroll to be kept with a Baroque violin when bringing its neck into conformance with modern standards.

Strings were first made of sheep gut (commonly known as catgut, which despite the name, did not come from cats), or simply gut, which was stretched, dried, and twisted. In the early years of the 20th century, strings were made of either gut or steel. Modern strings may be gut, solid steel, stranded steel, or various synthetic materials such as perlon, wound with various metals, and sometimes plated with silver. Most E strings are unwound, either plain or plated steel. Gut strings are not as common as they once were, but many performers use them to achieve a specific sound especially in historically informed performance of Baroque music. Strings have a limited lifetime. Eventually, when oil, dirt, corrosion, and rosin accumulate, the mass of the string can become uneven along its length. Apart from obvious things, such as the winding of a string coming undone from wear, players generally change a string when it no longer plays "true" (with good intonation on the harmonics), losing the desired tone, brilliance and intonation. String longevity depends on string quality and playing intensity.

A violin is tuned in fifths, in the notes G3, D4, A4, E5. The lowest note of a violin, tuned normally, is G3, or G below middle C (C4). (On rare occasions, the lowest string may be tuned down by as much as a fourth, to D3.) The highest note is less well defined: E7, the E two octaves above the open string (which is tuned to E5) may be considered a practical limit for orchestral violin parts,but it is often possible to play higher, depending on the length of the fingerboard and the skill of the violinist. Yet higher notes (up to C8) can be sounded by stopping the string, reaching the limit of the fingerboard, and/or by using artificial harmonics.

CHAPTER FOURTEEN

Sexa phone

The saxophone (referred to colloquially as the sax) is a type of single-reed woodwind instrument with a conical body, usually made of brass. As with all single-reed instruments, sound is produced when a reed on a mouthpiece vibrates to produce a sound wave inside the instrument's body. The pitch is controlled by opening and closing holes in the body to change the effective length of the tube.The holes are closed by leather pads attached to keys operated by the player. Saxophones are made in various sizes and are almost always treated as transposing instruments. Saxophone players are called saxophonists.

The saxophone is used in a wide range of musical styles including classical music (such as concert bands, chamber music, solo repertoire, and occasionally orchestras), military bands, marching bands, jazz (such as big bands and jazz combos), and contemporary music. The saxophone is also used as a solo and melody instrument or as a member of a horn section in some styles of rock and roll and popular music.

The saxophone was invented by the Belgian instrument maker Adolphe Sax in the early 1840s[3] and was patented on 28 June 1846. Sax invented two groups of seven instruments each—one group contained instruments in C and F, and the other group contained instruments in B♭ and E♭. The B♭ and E♭ instruments soon became dominant, and most saxophones encountered today are from this series. Instruments from the series pitched in C and F never gained a foothold and constituted only a small fraction of instruments made by Sax. High-pitch (also marked "H" or "HP") saxophones tuned sharper than the (concert) A = 440 Hz standard were produced into the early twentieth century for sonic qualities suited for outdoor use, but are not playable to modern tuning and are considered obsolete. Low-pitch (also marked "L" or "LP") saxophones are equivalent in tuning to modern instruments. C soprano and C melody saxophones were produced for the casual market as parlor instruments during the early twentieth century, and saxophones in F were introduced during the late 1920s but never gained acceptance. The modern saxophone family consists entirely of B♭ and E♭ instruments.

The pitch of a saxophone is controlled by opening or closing the tone holes along the body of the instrument to change the length of the vibrating air column. The tone holes are closed by leather pads connected to keys—most are operated by the player's fingers, but some are operated using the palm or the side of a finger. There is an octave key, which raises the pitch of the lower notes by one octave. The lowest possible note, with all of the pads closed, is the (written) B♭ below middle C. Modern baritone saxophones are commonly constructed to play a low A, and a small number of altos keyed to low A have also been manufactured. The highest keyed note has traditionally been the F two and a half octaves above the low B♭, but higher-quality instruments now have an extra key for a high F♯, and a high G key can be found on some modern soprano saxophones. Notes above the keyed range are part of the altissimo register of the saxophone and can be produced using advanced embouchure techniques and fingering combinations. Saxophone music is written in treble clef (appropriately transposed for each different type of instrument) and all saxophones use the same key arrangement and fingerings, enabling players to switch between different types of saxophones fairly easily.

Soprano and sopranino saxophones are usually constructed with a straight tube with a flared bell at the end, although some are made in the curved shape of the other saxophones. Alto and larger saxophones have a detachable curved neck and a U-shaped bend (the bow) that directs the tubing upward as it approaches the bell. There are rare examples of alto, tenor, and baritone saxophones with mostly straight bodies

From the earliest days of the saxophone the body and key cups have been made from sheet brass stock, which can be worked into complex shapes. The keywork is manufactured from other types of brass stock. King made saxophones with necks and bells of sterling silver from the 1930s into the early 1960s. Yanagisawa revived this idea in the 1980s and later introduced instruments entirely made of sterling silver.

Keilwerth and P. Mauriat have used nickel silver, a copper-nickel-zinc alloy more commonly used for flutes, for the bodies of some saxophone models.For visual and tonal effect, higher copper variants of brass are sometimes substituted for the more common "yellow brass" and "cartridge brass." Yanagisawa made its 902 and 992 series saxophones with the high copper alloy phosphor bronze to achieve a darker, more "vintage" tone than the brass 901 and 991 models.

Other materials are used for some mechanical parts and keywork. Buttons where the fingers contact the keys are usually made from plastic or mother of pearl. Rods, screw pins, and springs are usually made of blued or stainless steel. Mechanical buffers of felt, cork, leather, and various synthetic materials are used to minimize mechanical noise from key movement and to optimize the action of the keywork. Nickel silver is sometimes used for hinges for its advantages of mechanical durability, although the most common material for such applications has remained brass.

Manufacturers usually apply a finish to the surface of the instrument's body and keywork. The most common finish is a thin coating of clear or colored acrylic lacquer to protect the brass from oxidation and maintain a shiny appearance. Silver or gold plating are offered as options on some models. Some silver plated saxophones are also lacquered. Plating saxophones with gold is an expensive process because an underplating of silver is required for the gold to adhere to.Nickel plating has been used on the bodies of early budget model saxophones and is commonly used on keywork when a more durable finish is desired, mostly with student model saxophones. Chemical surface treatment of the base metal has come into use as an alternative to the lacquer and plating finishes in recent years.

The saxophone uses a single-reed mouthpiece similar to that of the clarinet. Each size of saxophone (alto, tenor, etc.) uses a different size of reed and mouthpiece.

Most saxophonists use reeds made from Arundo donax cane, but since the middle of the twentieth century some have been made of fiberglass or other composite materials. Saxophone reeds are proportioned slightly differently from clarinet reeds, being wider for the same length. Commercial reeds vary in hardness and design, and single-reed players try different reeds to find those that suit their mouthpiece, embouchure, and playing style.

Mouthpiece design has a profound impact on tone.[10] Different mouthpiece design characteristics and features tend to be favored for different styles. Early mouthpieces were designed to produce a "warm" and "round" sound for classical playing. Among classical mouthpieces, those with a concave ("excavated") chamber are more true to Adolphe Sax's original design; these provide a softer or less piercing tone favored by the Raschèr school of classical playing. Saxophonists who follow the French school of classical playing, influenced by Marcel Mule, generally use mouthpieces with smaller chambers for a somewhat "brighter" sound with relatively more upper harmonics. The use of the saxophone in dance orchestras and jazz ensembles from the 1920s onward placed emphasis on dynamic range and projection, leading to innovation in mouthpiece designs. At the opposite extreme from the classical mouthpieces are those with a small chamber and a low clearance above the reed between the tip and the chamber, called high baffle. These produce a bright sound with maximum projection, suitable for having a sound stand out among amplified instruments.

Mouthpieces come in a wide variety of materials including vulcanized rubber (sometimes called hard rubber or ebonite), plastic and metals like bronze or surgical steel. Less common materials that have been used include wood, glass, crystal, porcelain and bone. Recently, Delrin has been added to the stock of mouthpiece materials.

The effect of mouthpiece materials on tone of the saxophone has been the subject of much debate. According to Larry Teal, the mouthpiece material has little, if any, effect on the sound, and the physical dimensions give a mouthpiece its tone color

The saxophone was designed around 1840 by Adolphe Sax, a Belgian instrument maker, flautist, and clarinetist. Born in Dinant and originally based in Brussels, he moved to Paris in 1842 to establish his musical instrument business. Before working on the saxophone, he made several improvements to the bass clarinet by improving its keywork and acoustics and extending its lower range. Sax was also a maker of the ophicleide, a large conical brass instrument in the bass register with keys similar to a woodwind instrument. His experience with these two instruments allowed him to develop the skills and technologies needed to make the first saxophones.

As an outgrowth of his work improving the bass clarinet, Sax began developing an instrument with the projection of a brass instrument and the agility of a woodwind. He wanted it to overblow at the octave, unlike the clarinet, which rises in pitch by a twelfth when overblown. An instrument that overblows at the octave has identical fingering for both registers.

Sax created an instrument with a single-reed mouthpiece and conical brass body. Having constructed saxophones in several sizes in the early 1840s, Sax applied for, and received, a 15-year patent for the instrument on 28 June 1846.The patent encompassed 14 versions of the fundamental design, split into two categories of seven instruments each, and ranging from sopranino to contrabass. A limited number of instruments in the series pitched in F and C were produced by Sax, but the series pitched in E ♭ and B ♭ quickly became the standard. All the instruments were given an initial written range from the B below the treble staff to the E ♭ one half-step below the third ledger line above staff, giving each saxophone a range of two and a half octaves. Sax's patent expired in 1866. Thereafter, numerous other instrument manufacturers implemented their own improvements to the design and keywork.

Sax's original keywork, which was based on the Triebert system 3 oboe for the left hand and the Boehm clarinet for the right, was simplistic and made certain legato passages and wide intervals extremely difficult to finger; that system would later evolve with extra keys, linkage mechanisms, and alternate fingerings to make some intervals less difficult.

Early in the development of the saxophone the upper keyed range was extended to E, then F above the staff; 1880s era sheet music for saxophone was written for the range of low B to F. In 1887 the Buffet-Crampon company obtained a patent for extending the bell and adding an extra key to extend the range downwards by one semitone to B ♭ .This extension is standard in modern designs, with the notable exception of baritone saxophones keyed to low A. The upper range to F would remain the standard for nearly a century until a high F ♯ key became common on modern saxophones.

In a rare early inclusion in an orchestral score, the saxophone was used in Gioacchino Rossini's Robert Bruce (1846)

In the 1840s and 1850s, Sax's invention gained use in small classical ensembles (both all-saxophone and mixed), as a solo instrument, and in French and British military bands. Saxophone method books were published and saxophone instruction was offered at conservatories in France, Switzerland, Belgium, Spain, and Italy. By 1856 the French Garde Republicaine band included eight saxophones, making it the largest ensemble to prominently feature the instrument. The saxophone was used experimentally in orchestral scores, but never came into widespread use as an orchestral instrument. In 1853-54 the orchestra of Louis Antoine Jullien featured a soprano saxophone on a concert tour of the United States.

After an early period of interest and support from classical music communities in Europe, their interest in the instrument waned in the late nineteenth century. Saxophone teaching at the Paris Conservatory was suspended from 1870 to 1900 and classical saxophone repertoire stagnated during that period.But it was during this same period that the saxophone began to be promoted in the United States, largely through the efforts of Patrick Gilmore, leader of the 22nd Regiment band, and Edward A. Lefebre, a Dutch emigre and saxophonist with family business associations with Sax. Lefebre settled in New York in early 1872 after he arrived as a clarinetist with a British opera company. Gilmore organized the World Peace Jubilee and International Music Festival taking place in Boston that summer. The Garde Republicaine band performed and Lefebre was a clarinetist with the Great Festival Orchestra for that event.In the fall of 1873 Gilmore was reorganizing the 22nd Regiment band under the influence of the Garde Republicaine band and recruited Lefebre, who had established a reputation in New York as a saxophonist over the previous year. Gilmore's band soon featured a soprano-alto-tenor-baritone saxophone section, which also performed as a quartet. The Gilmore-Lefebre association lasted until Gilmore's death in 1892, during which time Lefebre also performed in smaller ensembles of various sizes and instrumentation, and worked with composers to increase light classical and popular repertoire for saxophone.

Lefebre's later promotional efforts were extremely significant in broadening adoption of the saxophone. Starting towards the end of the 1880s he consulted with the brass instrument manufacturer C.G. Conn to develop and start production of improved saxophones to replace the costly, scantly available, and mechanically unreliable European instruments in the American market. The early 1890s saw regular production of saxophones commence at Conn and its offshoot Buescher Manufacturing Company, which dramatically increased availability of saxophones in the US. Lefebre worked with the music publisher Carl Fischer to distribute his transcriptions, arrangements, and original works for saxophone, and worked with the Conn Conservatory to further saxophone pedagogy in the US. Lefebre's associations with Conn and Fischer lasted into the first decade of the twentieth century and Fischer continued to publish new arrangements of Lefebre's works posthumously.